普通高等教育"十二五"规划教材

留美学习与生活
情景对话 上册

学习篇
Fly Away

（美）Michael Kussmaul　杜曾慧◎主编

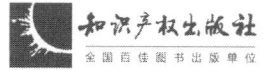

全国百佳图书出版单位

内容提要

本书分为上下两册,重点注重于语言的运用能力,为读者构建了一个个实际的语言情景,每章都是以场景的形式出现,有知识类的介绍,词汇总结、相应的话题讨论,和典型情景对话范例,既适合阅读者自己阅读学习,也适合用于英语教学。本书上册为学习篇,主要致力于出国前的各项准备及新生入学后的注意事项。例如,如何申请国外大学,国际航班注意事项、新生入校后如何参加学校的各项活动及其注意事项等;下册为生活篇,主要致力于学校的课外活动,生活上可能遇见的问题及如何处理这些问题。如美国钱币知识的介绍,学生证及护照、在学校餐厅和校外就餐等生活常识。

责任编辑: 于晓菲 许波　　**责任出版:** 陆运霞 刘译文

图书在版编目(CIP)数据

留美学习与生活情景对话(上、下)-Fly Away/(美)Michael Kussmaul,杜曾慧主编.—北京:知识产权出版社,2013.04
　　ISBN 978-7-5130-1932-3
　　Ⅰ.①F… Ⅱ.①杜… Ⅲ.①留学教育-英语 Ⅳ.①H31
　　中国版本图书馆 CIP 数据核字(2013)第 046647 号

留美学习与生活情景对话(上)(学习篇)——Fly Away
LIUMEI XUEXI YU SHENGHUO QINGJING DUIHUA (SHANG) (XUEXIPIAN)

(美) Michael Kussmaul　　杜曾慧　主编

出版发行:	知识产权出版社			
社　　址:	北京市海淀区马甸南村1号	邮　编:	100088	
网　　址:	http://www.ipph.cn	邮　箱:	rqyuxiaofei@163.com	
发行电话:	010-82000893 转 8101	传　真:	010-82005070/82000893	
责编电话:	010-82000860 转 8363	责编邮箱:	yuxiaofei@cnipr.com	
印　　刷:	北京中献拓方科技发展有限公司	经　销:	新华书店及相关销售网点	
开　　本:	720mm×960mm　1/16	印　张:	20.25(上、下册)	
版　　次:	2013年4月第1版	印　次:	2013年4月第1次	
字　　数:	308千字(上、下册)	定　价:	42.00元(上、下册)	

ISBN 978-7-5130-1932-3/H・099(4775)

出版权专有　侵权必究
如有印装质量问题,本社负责调换。

《留美学习与生活情景对话（学习篇）——Fly Away》编委会

主　编：（美）Michael Kussmaul　杜曾慧

副主编：严　峻　　陆　杨　　黄静雅　　王　静

序

本书的编写旨在帮助即将出国留学的学生做好留学前的准备工作。如对学校的申请，出国前行程的准备，西方的教学体制等问题。

全书以全英文模拟情景的方式，针对在国外学习和生活时可能遇到的困难和解决途径，西方传统文化等问题进行了实际的模拟情景。通过一系列的模拟训练，使有出国学习意愿的学生能够提前了解西方的教学体制和文化，为学生出国后能够独立在国外生存和学习打下基础。同时也使得不准备出国学习的学生了解这方面知识，使他们能得到全面的基本技能训练。培养学生准确地理解语言、正确地运用语言的能力，达到丰富学生的语言表达，强化学生的语言能力的目的，重点培养学生逻辑思维的能力，增强其国际视野，使其能够更全面了解中西方文化差异。

本书编写的基本指导原则是"以应用为目的，实用为主，够用为度"。本书英文的编写合作者为资深美籍教师 Michael Kusssmaul 博士，近十年来，他分别在五个国家从事雅思英语教学工作近十年，在 30 个国家任过教师，曾经凭借出色的教学水平获得过吉林省政府颁发的"友谊"奖。本书所有英文部分均得到他的认可和审查，均为原创。

本书分为上下两册，重点注重于语言的运用能力，为读者构建了一个个实际的语言情景，每章都是以场景的形式出现，有知识类的介绍、词汇总结、相应的话题讨论，和典型情景对话范例，既适合阅读者自己阅读学习，也适合用于英语教学。本书上册为学习篇，主要致力于出国前的各项准备及新生入学后的注意事项。例如，如何申请国外大学，国际航班注意事项、新生入校后如何参加学校的各项活动及其注意事项等；下册为生活篇，主要致力于学校的课外活动，生活上可能遇见的问题及如何处理这些问题。如美国钱币知识的介绍，学生证及护照、在学校餐厅和校外就餐等生活常识。

  本书所有章节均以英文书写为主，均为原创，非常地道，原汁原味，同时配有适当的中文说明，显得浅显易懂。在每一章都配有相应的场景对话，能对学生在留学过程中碰到问题后如何解决有很大的帮助。本书适用于学生自学，同时也可以作为相关英语教师进行课堂训练的素材。

  本书由杜曾慧和 Michael Kussmaul 博士担任主编，在编写的过程中得到了高等教育学会和知识产权出版社有关人员的大力支持和帮助，在此我们表示诚挚的谢意。由于时间仓促，书中难免存在不足之处，真诚地欢迎各位同仁批评指正，如有意见、建议请通过下面的 E-Mail 联系我们：duzh@niit.edu.cn

（美）Michael Kussmaul 杜曾慧

2013 年 1 月

Table of Contents

Introduction 内容介绍 /1

Chapter 1   Preparing to Depart

　　　　　　准备出发 /5

Chapter 2   Arriving and Settling in

　　　　　　到了，安顿下来吧 /31

Chapter 3   Orientation and Scheduling/Choosing Classes

　　　　　　新生入学教育 / 新生如何选课 /47

Chapter 4   Getting around the Campus

　　　　　　熟悉校园 /67

Chapter 5   Study Tips for University Success

　　　　　　学业取得成功的小窍门 /89

Appendix A – Dialogues   学习场景对话攻略 /111

Appendix B – Tables & Forms   各类申请表格 /129

Appendix B – Word Bank   词汇表 /137

Introduction
内容介绍

Guided Reading

  每年成千上万的中国学生因为各种原因出国学习，本指南为你提供了如何准备前往目的国、如何获取到您所选学校的信息、当您到达机场怎么办、如何让您通过海关、到了你所选择的大学或学院后又该做些什么等方面的信息。来吧，跟我们一起体验真正的海外留学生活吧！

Every year, thousands of Chinese students go abroad to study and learn. They all go for various reasons. Some go to learn a new language, while others go to further their education. Whatever the reason, studying abroad is something that will enhance your life and have a profound effect on you forever. Not everyone can go abroad, but for those who can, this guide will help you out.

The purpose of this guide is to give you much needed information about preparing to travel outside China and what to expect when you arrive at the school you've chosen. We will also look at what to do when you arrive at the airport, how to get you through customs and what to do when you finally get to the college or university.

As you take this journey, we will give you phrases that might make things easier for you in a foreign land. There will be some dialogues for you to practice so that you can be ready for just about anything. We will also offer some words of wisdom that you should pay close attention to. These thoughts will help you at any time. In the back of this guide, you will find an appendix (A) that contains useful information that you can refer to when you need it. A second appendix (B) will give you practical terminology that can be used in all types of situations.

Students travel abroad every year. They have a variety of stories to tell when they have returned, but most of them will tell anyone that they had a great time and learned a lot. We hope your journey will be filled with good times, wonderful memories and all branches of knowledge. Bon voyage!

Vocabulary

enhance [in'hɑ:ns] vt. 提高，增加，加强

profound [prə'faund] adj. 深奥的，渊博的，极度的，意义深远的

effect [i'fekt] n. 影响

wisdom ['wizdəm] n. 智慧，明智，才智，聪明，至理名言

appendix [ə'pendiks] n. 附录

terminology [tə:mi'nɔlədʒi, tə:mə'nɔlədʒi] n. 术语

guide [gaid] n. 指导者；向导；导游

purpose ['pə·pəs] n. 意志；目的；作用

journey ['dʒə·ni] n. 旅行，旅程行期；历程，过程

phrases [freiziz] n. ＜语＞短语（phrase 的名词复数）；成语；说法

practice ['præktis] vi. 实行；练习

situation [ˌsitju'eiʃən] n.（人的）情况；局面

variety [və'raiiti] n. 多样；种类；杂耍；变化，多样化

memories ['meməriz] n. 记忆力（memory 的名词复数）；记忆中的事物；记忆系统；记忆容量

knowledge ['nɔlidʒ] n. 知识

Bon voyage [ˌbɔnvɔi'ɑ:dʒ] ＜法＞再见，一路顺风（平安）

Chapter 1
Preparing to Depart

准备出发

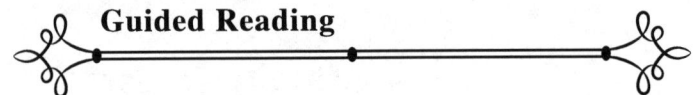

Guided Reading

准备出发了!看看我们应该做哪些方面的准备吧。这章将告诉你临行前应该准备哪些文书方面的工作和每一件事情的时间期限,如何填写申请表,准备成绩单,到外国大使馆面试要做哪些准备等等。

Okay, so you've decided to go abroad and study. Great! In order to leave the country you must have a lot of paperwork completed so that no problems come up as you travel. This section will look at what kinds of paperwork you need to complete, and if possible, the deadlines for completing them. Please keep in mind that all foreign countries have their own rules for handling student paperwork. Please consult the website of the college or university you wish to attend and make sure you have completed all the required paperwork for them. Since you will be considered as an "International Student", all colleges and universities will have specific guidelines for you to follow. They will ask for a completed application, which can usually be completed online to save unnecessary paperwork, and request that you send them your transcripts of the classes you have taken.

Application 申请事宜

The application for any college or university is quite simple to complete. If you are not sure what you must fill in, a short e-mail to the school with a few direct questions will solve your problems. The best way to fill out the application is to print a copy of the form, fill it out as completely as possible, and then go back to the website and fill in the application online. This way you will save time and unnecessary mistakes. If you have a printed copy of the application and still need some help, you can ask foreign a teacher to help you.

What information should you fill in the application form? Your name, date of birth, a home address, passport number and visa number, etc. Additional items would be email address, home telephone number and usually a second number in case of emergencies. The school will ask you

about your major field of study. You should take your time and look over what the school offers and choose a major that you feel can benefit you.

这是一份申请表，一起来填一填吧！

表一　入学申请表

ADMISSION SECTION PRINT CLEARLY IN BLACK INK					
Name of Institution	City/Province	Country	Dates Attended From To	Graduation Date

Social Security Number _____ Your Social Security Number will be a student identifier. Please enter it here if you have one.

Full Legal Name _____

Permanent Address _____

City _____ Country/State _____ ZIP _____

County/Province _____ Date of Birth _____

Phone Cell _____

Receive text messages from University? Yes o　No o　Email _____

Program Type	Ethnicity and Race*
New freshman	Are you Hispanic/Latino? Yes o No o
Transfer with less than 24 semester hours	Choose appropriate race. Check all that apply.
Transfer student	American Indian/Alaskan Native
Postgraduate (degree seeking)	Asian
High school concurrent	Native Hawaiian or Other Pacific Islander
Transient (visiting student)	Black or African-American

National Student Exchange   White
Non degree seeking   Not disclosed
Mr. o   Mrs. o   Ms. o   Dr. o
Parent/Guardian/Spouse Contact _____
Relationship_____ Phone_____
Address _____
City_____ Country/State _____ ZIP _____
Email _____
Cell phone _____ Receive text messages from University? Yes o   No o
Student's Full Name

_____   _____
          Last or family name   Given name
MI   Social Security Number (if available)
List High School or Prep School
List all high schools attended. Grades or marks are needed for years 9–12 and beyond.
Name_____
Address _____

Dates attended _____   _____
From   To
Graduation _____
date
List courses to be completed during your senior year of high school (freshmen only). (The University course requirements are a factor in the admissions process.)
Have you previously enrolled at this university? Yes o   No o
Student number_____
LIST ALL COLLEGES ATTENDED OR THAT YOU PLAN TO ATTEND BEFORE ENROLLING AT THIS UNIVERSITY.
Attach an additional sheet if necessary. An official transcript from each college must be submitted to the Admissions Office at the university.
Note: If there is a break of more than one term in your education, please attach a statement of activity.
If you answer yes to any of the following questions, please attach a separate sheet of

paper stating the approximate date and explaining the circumstances of each incident.

DISCIPLINARY/CRIMINAL HISTORY

1. Have you ever been found responsible for a disciplinary violation, academic or behavioral, at a college, university or other postsecondary institution which resulted in your probation, suspension, removal, dismissal or expulsion? Yes o No o

2. Have you ever been convicted of, pled guilty to or pled no contest to a felony or sexual offense? Yes o No o

3. Are you currently the subject of pending charges or an indictment, or subject to arrest, for any criminal offense, including felonies or lesser offenses? Yes o No o

4. At the time of your entry to UA, will you have been separated from the U.S. Armed Forces, National Guard or Reserves with a dishonorable or bad conduct discharge or been dismissed by sentence of a general court-martial or sentenced to confinement adjudged by a court-martial or in a federal or state penitentiary or correctional institution? Yes o No o

I certify that I have complied with the provisions of the United States Military Selective Service Act (50 U.S.C. App 453) by registering with the Selective Service Board or that I am not yet 18 years of age and I will register when required or that I am not required by law to register. (This certification is required by State of Alabama Legislative Act 91-584.) I certify that all information given in this application is complete and accurate. I understand that withholding information requested or giving false information may make me ineligible for admission and enrollment or subject to suspension.

Capstone Creed: As a member of the University of Alabama community, I will pursue knowledge; act with fairness, honesty, and respect;

foster individual and civic responsibility; and strive for excellence.

Applicant's signature (full legal name) _____

The application posted above is only part of a complete application. This section is usually called "Personal Data Information." When you fill out your application for school, you are required to complete everything. This means you fill in every blank on the application. Since this is time-consuming, it is best to print up a copy of the application and fill it out completely before you attempt to do so online. Personal Data is information about you. The information you give to the school will be registered and a file will be generated with your name on it. This file will contain all the paperwork you have submitted to the university, all classes you have taken and all financial information such as banking, scholarships and/or financial assistance. The application, after it has been submitted to the university, will also generate a student number for you. This number will be used by you for the time you are at the university. There will be more information about the student number later in this section. When filling out an application for a school in an English-speaking country, use English at all times. Use pinyin when you need to write your name. You will also use it when you sign your application. Do not sign it in Chinese.

Numbers are a critical part of the application. Most Chinese students know their numbers, but they are not very good at writing them in English. Here is what the numbers should look like:

      1 2 3 4 5 6 7 8 9 10

Permanent address would be your parent's address, not your address at school. All information from the university will go to your permanent address unless you tell them differently. Your address at school would be considered as a temporary address. If your permanent address has a P.O. Box number, this means you pick up your mail at the local China Post, and the mail is not delivered to your home. P. O. stands for Post Office. Your ad-

dress is very important and it must be complete or you might not get your mail from the university. The street address should have the following items in it:

House number – a number listed on the outside of the building.

If you live in an apartment building, you would write down the building number and your apartment number in the address.

The city in which you live. For example, Nanjing.

The province in which you live. For example, Jiangsu

The country in which you live. For example, China.

The postal code for the city in which you live. For example, NIIT is 210046.

Email is the best way to contact you. Universities have been part of the electronic age for a while and they prefer to use email since it means less paperwork for them. So your email should be written carefully and clearly. Any little error will result in missing the information you need from the university. Many times, universities will ask new students to fill their email address in the online application twice, so that there is no mistake. So be very careful when writing your email address.

Program Type tells the Admissions Office where to place you in terms of status. You could be a transfer student moving from one college to another, a freshman just entering college out of high school, or a transient student or Visiting student. This section is not difficult to figure out. All you need to do is to check the appropriate box for your student status.

Ethnicity and Race is designed according to Federal Law. Schools should have a diverse student body, and according to the law, they must enroll all ethnic groups. This section provides information to the US Government about the percentage of students enrolled in the university. Since you are Chinese, you would check the Asian box.

The next section of the application is called "Contact Information". This section is primarily for your parents. You need to fill in the name of your mother or father, the home address, telephone number and email address. The university will use this information if something happens to you while abroad. They will also use this address to send your grades home while you are on vacation and away from the university. Any pertinent information that the school wants to inform you will be sent to this address. For example, during summer vacation, you might be at home relaxing and you will get information from the school telling you when to enroll for the fall semester classes. The school will also inform you when you should return to the school to begin classes. So this address is important for both you and the university.

The section that follows the Contact Information is Education History. This section will give the university a better idea about you as a student. You should list your high school, but not your middle school. University Admissions only wants your high school information if you are enrolled as a freshman. If you are transferring from another college you can list your high school and the date you graduated on the application. The more important information is the number of classes you have taken and your grades of the classes. This is where you send a transcript of classes you have completed. The transcript should be in two forms: one in English, one in Chinese. Both should be stamped by the appropriate officer at your school. The university will use the English version of your transcripts to decide how many credits you can successfully transfer and how many you will need to graduate from their program. Please see the portion of this section entitled transcripts for more information.

Another part of the application process is the Processing Fee. This is a single payment that must accompany the application in order for the school to process it. The fee proves that you are serious about attending their institution. As you move into higher levels of education, the application fee will increase. So what kind of information is in the application? Well, they want to know your name and a few things about you. They also want to know your grades at your current school, if you have taken the required tests (IELTS, TOEFL, GRE, GMAT, etc.) and what you scored. On the application there are many sections that you must fill in. You must send a resume, grades, reference letters and test scores.

If you are going to a foreign school right after high school, do not worry too much about your major field of study. If you are not sure, you can always tell them that you are undecided. If you are transferring from a college or university to a foreign school, you need to tell them your major field of study so they can match the classes you have already taken with the classes that they offer. If your classes do not match up with the foreign school's curriculum, you might have to take additional classes once you arrive at the school. If you have graduated from a college or university in China and wish to pursue your graduate degree, you will need to do many additional things before you can study in a foreign school. One item required is an essay. The foreign school will give you a topic and you must write an essay no longer than 1,500 words, on that topic. The essay is submitted when you send your application to the school. Some universities will require two essays on two different topics. Each school has its own requirements for admission into its graduate programs.

One of the major items you must complete when filling out the application is the Reference Section. You should have at least two people submit references about you. Both parties should be considered 'professional' with a title, such as Doctor, Professor, Manager, etc. attached to their name. Most foreign schools require the references be sent separately by the referees, not by the student. When submitting an application online, the reference section merely asks you to submit the names of the people writing your letters of reference, their email addresses and their titles. Once the information has been entered, the school will send an email to each person you listed and they will submit their letter of reference about you.

怎样写留学申请书

在准备留学申请材料时，作为对外联系主要文件之一的简历，其质量高低将直接影响申请者的成功率，为了能让对方清晰地了解申请者，简历在写作方面应力求真实、全面、简洁、明了。

留学申请者的简历应包括以下几个方面的内容：

1. 姓名：与各种学历证明的姓名相同，如有更改姓名的情况，务必在公证时予以声明，并附上公证书。

2. 性别

3. 出生年月日及地点。与各类学历证明的出生年月日一致，出生地点写明国别和省份。

4. 国籍

5. 婚否

6. 现在工作单位及详细通信地址。

7. 个人教育背景。包括大学、硕士阶段的在读时间，所在大学的名称、专业和所获学位，参加工作后的受教育经历，主要指脱产接受专门的进修、培训或学习。

8. 个人从事专业的经历。填写专业经历应力求抓住重点，突出研究方向。担任教学工作的可列出主讲、助讲课程的名称，担任研究工作的可列出参加各个研究项目的课题名称。

9. 个人的著作、论文或研究成果要分门别类列出，并一定要与个人专业经历相一致。所列著作要注明名称、出版年月、出版单位。所列论文要注明论文题目、刊载杂志或期刊名称、期号、语种。对于在学术会议上发表的文章还要注明学术会议的名称、召开时间和地点等。如果其中有被外国学者评论过的，最好附上刊载评论文章的杂志名称及时间。

10. 外语水平。注明参加 TEF、TOEFL、GRE 等考试的时间、地点及成绩。若申请者掌握多门外语，则要一一注明语种并说明熟练程度。

11. 参加何种学术团体，得到何种荣誉。学术团体一般应是省、市或行业一级以下的专业学术团体，在学术团体中所担任的职务可加以注明。荣誉主要是指在专业、技术研究方面获得的奖励和荣誉，并要注明获奖名称、颁奖时间和颁奖单位。

12. 拟申请的大学和导师的姓名。可根据申请者查询的资料予以注明，并要注意按照每个单位、每位导师一份简历的原则，即在同一份简历中不必注明全部想要联系的单位和导师。

13. 拟进行的研究方向和希望从事研究的题目。国外院校的专业面一般较宽，要根据国外情况，力求专业面与其一致。研究课题可根据自己的研究兴趣和需要，同时也要尽量考虑对方的条件。

在简历的书写过程中申请者还应注意必须尽力保持字迹的工整、清楚，最好用打印机打印。一份成功简历的秘诀在于：既不要言过其实，又必须充分反映自己的实际水平。

An example: This would be considered a Personal Essay by the student.

Due to the comprehensiveness of China's "reform and opening up" policy, economics plays an increasingly important role in the development of its global position. Though more and more companies were built, the management cannot catch up with the development of themselves. Management is a burgeoning field in China, so I hope I can acquire more modern knowledge on it in England.

The roots of my strong interest in business can be traced back to my childhood. My father was among the first of China's new breed of modern entrepreneurs. As a young girl, it was inspirational when hearing about his business ventures, and meeting the varied and interesting circle of entrepreneurs. My mother was also involved in business as an accountant, helping my father with simple calculations. And so it was early in my life that I hoped I, also, would someday be able to enter the realm of business. With time going by, I preferred reading books to satisfy my curiosity. I never ceased to contemplate over the questions I encountered. Subjects on business and management became special fascinations to me and my knowledge of psychology as well as interest in this field was increased rapidly.

As a high school student in China, I had to concentrate on the College Entrance Examination (CEE), even so, general reading has never excluded from my life. Unfortunately, when sitting in the CEE exam in June, 2001, I was so nervous that I didn't score well. I enrolled in the department of Computer Science in Zhejiang College of Traditional Chinese Medicine. Any attempt to persuade myself to focus on my major turned out to be a failure at the beginning of my college life. After several terms, I realized that I would never be interested in being a programmer or an engineer. At that moment, I lost my direction and objectives.

My persistence in reading saved me from the dark situation. As a matter of fact, I enjoyed reading books including Encyclopedia American, and some books about management by Peter F. Drucker. I began to notice something interesting: Why some companies can produce more than others? Why some company can sell more than others? Why some companies can build up but others cannot when facing the same difficulties?

With the questions in my mind, I started to read many relevant books. I was lucky to read the book *Jack: Straight from the Gut* by Jack Welch, in Which John A. Byrne makes a clear illustration that the management is important for a company. When I was a junior, I ran a bookshop by myself near my school. I should manage not only the finance but also the employees in my shop even made some strategies to enlarge the business to hold on the operation of the shop. From this, my interpersonal skills and the capacity in business has been greatly developed, definitely I was increasingly interested in what I was doing. By December, 2003, I had finally determined to take business management as my career instead of IT. To accumulate more relevant knowledge, I strived to gain more practical work experience in some big companies.

Fortunately, as a senior, I began by conducting an internship in an architecture company in Zhejiang province. Over six months, I worked as an assistant of the manager to harmonize the relationship between the different departments in this company and to draft some management system, which broadened my perspective of management conditions and business performance in different industries. The experience showed me that management is much more important than that I thought in big companies. After graduation, I continued my work in this company. In May, 2005, the company offered me an opportunity to participate in an training program held by a famous management school. Through in-depth discussions with teachers and students in the classes, they all encouraged me to pursue my future study in management field because of my intelligente and the brand new ideas I mentioned.

During the short period of training, I realized that pursuing a higher degree in management is a wise choice for me now. Lancaster, with its excellence in management, represents the perfect fit for my needs. In the challenging environment, I can build the required foundation of knowledge related to management to achieve my goals. I am firmly convinced that your admission will be my first step of success. With this in mind, I hereby submit my application, and await your favorable reply.

Transcripts 成绩单

Any student wishing to study in a foreign country must submit transcripts of his or her classes. The foreign school requires original, stamped documents from your school that prove you have taken the classes. Most foreign schools will ask you to send them English versions of the transcripts. If this is not possible, they will charge you a fee to have your transcripts translated into English. In the U.S., most schools send their documents to a company in Minnesota for translation. The current cost for translation is $100 dollars. Transcripts can be scanned and downloaded as an attachment to the application. If this is not sufficient for the foreign school, they will request actual paper documents that you must send via postal service, DHL or FedEx. However, technology makes the application so much easier and efficient, most schools are okay with the electronic versions of your transcripts.

Speaking Test at Foreign Embassy/Consulate
在外国大使馆／领事馆的口语面试

All students wanting to study in an English-speaking country must take an interview at the Embassy or Consulate office for that country. The only exception to this rule is the UK. They do not require an interview. The interview is quite simple. You stand before an official representative of the government and they ask you questions. What do they ask? Here are a few questions you are likely to be asked when you go to the interview:

What is your name?

What will you study at school?

How long do you plan to stay in the country?

Do you have your letter of invitation from the school with you?

The letter of invitation is your acceptance letter to study at the school. You will need to bring this with you when you are interviewed as proof that you will study in the country. Also, the letter allows you to get your student visa so you can enter the country safely. The visa will be granted after you have completed the interview. The representative will prepare your visa and place it in your passport. To be on the safe side, make sure you bring along several passport-size photographs because they will be used on all documents with your name on them. If you are not sure how many you should bring, simply go to the website of the Embassy or Consulate and find out the answer. They have a section for student visas. You should be able to download the visa application and fill it out before submitting an online version to the Embassy or Consulate. All instructions should be clear and easy to follow. If you have a difficult time with it, find a foreign teacher to help you complete the forms.

赴美签证申请步骤：

第一步确定签证申请类别

根据自己的赴美目的和身份，确定所要申请的美国签证类别。

第二步确定领区范围

上海总领事馆领区：上海、浙江、江苏、安徽

有关领区的说明：指申请人的常住地，例如您的户籍在北京，但您主要在上海工作和居住，这种情况下您应该到上海总领事馆递交申请。如果您的常住地与您

的户籍所在地（亦即护照签发地）不是同一个省份的话，须在面试时向签证官说明，并提供相关证明，如暂住证或其他有关居住的证明。

如果是申请美国移民签证，不分户籍所在地，统一到广州领事馆办理。

自2004年3月3日后，美国非移民签证采用话务中心服务。该话务中心此项服务为"用户付费"性质，从2004年3月19日起，所有现在能交纳赴美签证申请费的中信实业银行将开始出售一种预先付款的加密电话卡，用该卡可启动签证信息话务中心的服务，获得签证信息并预约签证面谈时间。预先付费的加密电话卡每张售价为54元人民币，将允许持卡人使用话务中心12分钟的服务。首次通话后的剩余分钟可留待日后使用。若超时，需另购54元人民币的电话卡。

话务中心的付费方式有：信用卡、借记卡、银行汇票和邮政汇款。如使用信用卡或借记卡付费，用户在拨通预约电话后按录音指令输入你的信用卡或借记卡号码。亦可通过银行汇票或邮政汇款方式付费（因需要等待至少10天资料输入系统而不推荐使用）。该中心不接受个人支票。

拥有加密电话卡后，打电话至签证信息话务中心来预约面试时间，切记勿再打电话给美国使馆及领馆做预约。签证信息话务中心的电话号码是：4008-872-333。工作时间：星期一至星期五：上午7:00-下午7:00，星期六：上午8:00-下午5:00。

如果你在中国大陆以外打电话，请拨86-21-3881-4611（请注意国际长途电话费用将完全由致电者负担）签证信息话务中心同时提供签证咨询服务。

尽早预约。鉴于签证审核要求的增加和手续办理时间的延长，美领馆签证处建议所有申请人应根据个人行程安排，尽量提前申请。

签证材料的准备

按照自己的签证预约时间，一般预约早上8点面签。根据经验，学生可以提前30分钟进入使馆。根据笔者经验，进入时间越早，在使馆停留的时间会比较短，最佳时段是预约早上7点半的，最快早上9点前就可以出来了！

在进入使馆之前，需要注意您准备的签证申请材料。如果你是f1签证申请者，笔者在这儿给您提供一份材料清单，以供参考！

签证材料准备清单

1) 填写好，并附上照片的 ds 表格
2) 本人护照
3) 中信银行签证费收据（两张都要带上） 拿护照去中信银行买签证费
4) 网上缴纳 servies 费的收据 i-20 来了之后在网上交 200 美元
5) i-20 表原件
6) offer letter/admission letter 原件
7) 毕业证、学位证原件
8) 成绩单（尽量用密封的，不过非必须）
9) GRE/TOEFL 成绩单原件 申请高中要求 TOEFL/SSAT 成绩单（非必须）
10) 个人签证简历（高中和本科申请者不需要）
11) 父母工作收入证明
12) 银行存款证明
13) 其它辅助资产证明（如股票、证券、房产、汽车等）

现在不用这么详细，建议把房产证，和驾照带着就可以了

14) 未来学校 program 网页的介绍（非必须）

繁忙的签证大厅

进入大使馆、安检；递交指定申请材料，录入指纹；发放带颜色的牌子，后边排队；等待签证官叫号，面签。

提交制定申请材料，以 f1 签证申请者为例，ds-156、ds-157、ds-158 三套表格，学校 i-20、i-901 缴费收据，护照原件。一般建议申请者把这些东西装在一个口袋里边，这样会比较方便工作人员收取。

注意 ds-156 的第三页签证费的张贴方式。这个大家注意关注美国大使馆赴美签证页面关于表格的填写即可。

交完制定材料之后，开始录入指纹。双手除开拇指的所有手指录入，然后是两只手的拇指录取。确认完成之后，就可以发放有颜色的牌子做相关准备了！

注意左边正确的录入指纹的指示。

和签证官面谈，注意面谈时要面带微笑，双目直视对方，放轻松，只有你放松，VO才会放松。其实他们很累的，一天要给大约100多个人做面签，各种不同类型，所以请体谅一下。VO也是人。

随时准备提交自己准备的签证材料，我对学生的要求是遇到相关问题的时候及时出示相关材料加以证明。恭喜您！顺利获签，传说中的小"纸条"。上边需要填写您的姓名和面签日期，然后及时到大使馆指定的中国邮政办理护照邮寄回执。

Vocabulary

paperwork ['peipə.wə:k] n. 文书工作

deadlines ['dedlain] n. 最后期限，截止时间

consult [kən'sʌlt] v. 查阅，请教，商讨

request [ri'kwest] vt. 请求，要求

passport ['pɑ:s.pɔ:t] n. 护照

visa ['vi:zə] n. 签证

emergency [i'mə:dʒənsi] n. 突发事件，紧急状态

processing fee 加工费用

process ['prɑ:ses] v. 加工，处理，

accompany [ə'kʌmpəni] vt. 陪伴，伴随……发生，补充，给……伴奏

institution [.insti'tju:ʃən] n. 学校，机构

transferring [træns'fə:] v. 转移，调任，转乘

curriculum [kə'rikjuləm] n. 全部课程，课程

additional [ə'diʃənl] adj. 附加的，额外的

pursue [pə'sju:, pə'su:] v. 追求，追捕，继续执行，从事

graduate ['grædjueit] adj. 毕业的，获得学位的

essay ['esei, e'sei] n. 论文，短评，散文

submit [səb'mit] vt. 提交，递交

transcript ['trænskript] n. 成绩单

original [ə'ridʒənl] adj. 原始的，最初的，有独创性的，原版的

stamped [stæmpt] adj. 盖上邮戳的，盖章的

document ['dɔkjumənt] n. 文件，公文，文档

prove [pru:v] v. 证明，检验，结果是

electronic [ilek'trɔnik] adj. 电子的，电子学的

version ['və:ʃən] n. 版本，说法，译本，形式

Minnesota [mini'səutə] n. 明尼苏达（美国州名）
scan [skæn] vt. 扫描
attachment [ə'tætʃmənt] n. 附件，附属物
sufficient [sə'fiʃənt] adj. 足够的，充分的
actual ['æktʃuəl] adj. 实际的，事实上的
via ['vaiə] prep. 经由，通过
efficient [i'fiʒənt] adj. 效率高的，胜任的
exception [ik'sepʒən] n. 例外，不合规则
representative [repri'zentətiv] n. 代表
acceptance [ək'septəns] n. 认可，同意，承兑，接受
proof [pru:f] n. 证明，证据
student visa 学生签证
grant [grɑ:nt] v. 授予，同意，承认

Conversation Questions

Why do you want to study abroad?

What do your parents think about your going to another country?

Are you excited about going? Why?

What will you take with you when you leave China?

Can you tell me about the school you wish to attend?

What will be your major?

How long will you be away from China?

Have you filled out all the paperwork?

Did you take the IELTS or TOEFL exam?

When do you leave?

Discussion Questions

Many people want to study abroad, but some cannot. Why?

What will be the most difficult thing for you to overcome when you go to a new country?

Do you think the experience will be positive or negative for you? Why?

What are your goals?

Will you work in the other country while attending school? Where?

Practice Dialogues

Throughout this book you will have a variety of dialogues that you can use to practice speaking and ask questions. Each section of the book will have 3 dialogues for your use.

Dialogue #1 – Student and Embassy/Consulate Official

Officer: Hello, how are you today?

Student: I am fine. Thank you.

Officer: Good. Shall we get started?

Student: Okay, I am ready when you are.

Officer: Please tell me your full name.

Student: My name is _____.

Officer: Can you tell me where you were born?

Student: Yes, I was born in _____, in China.

Officer: And how old are you?

Student: I am _____ years old.

Officer: When will you be traveling abroad?

Student: I plan to leave during the summer, in July or August, before classes begin at the university.

Officer: What school will you be going to?

Student: I will be attending the University of _____.

Officer: And what will you study at the university?

Student: I will study _____.

Officer: How long will you be in the U.S.?

Student: I will be in the U.S. for 4 years unless I decide to get my Masters, too. Then I will be there for 6 years.

Officer: Very good. Thank you for your answers. I hope you have a safe trip and enjoy your time in the U.S.

Student: Thank you very much.

Dialogue # 2 – Two students talking

Student 1: So, are you ready for your big trip to the U.S.?

Student 2: Almost, but I feel like I am forgetting something.

Student 1: Did you make a list of all the things you need to take along?

Student 2: Yes, I have completed the list.

Student 1: Well, if you have any problems or you find that you left something behind, send me an email and I will send it to you.

Student 2: Oh that would be great. I don't know if I have forgotten something or if I am just nervous about the trip.

Student 1: I think you are just nervous about the trip.

Student 2: Yes, but I am also excited about it, too.

Student 1: Well, you should be. This is a once-in-a-lifetime opportunity.

Student 2: I know it is. And I am determining to make the most of it.

Student 1: You will do well and make lots of new friends when you get there.

Student 2: I have already made some new friends at the university. I was given their email addresses and I have been talking to them for 3 weeks now.

Student 1: That's great. So when you get there they will be waiting for you?

Student 2: Oh yes. They said they would pick me up at the airport after I go through Customs.

Student 1: Have you filled out all the paperwork for the university?

Student 2: Yes and no. I have sent almost everything to them, but I am waiting for my final grades here to send along to them. I told them the grades would be sent as soon as possible.

Student 1: Were they okay with that?

Student 2: Yes, they completely understand.

Student 1: Well, I will miss you so much. You must promise to write to me every week.

Student 2: I will. Plus we can chat from time to time on QQ or Skype.

Student 1: Okay. Now let's get you to the airport before you miss your flight.

Dialogue #3 – Student and Teacher

Teacher: Are you ready to go?

Student: I guess so. I have everything packed.

Teacher: When do you leave?

Student: I leave tomorrow morning at 9:15.

Teacher: How long will the flight be?

Student: They said it would take 12 hours.

Teacher: So you will arrive in the evening and you will be tired.

Student: Yes, after the plane lands they said it takes about 45 minutes to get through Customs and pick up the baggage.

Teacher: Will there be someone waiting for you?

Student: Yes, a few of the students from my dorm will meet me.

Teacher: That's good. Are you excited about the trip?

Student: Oh yes. I am very excited about it but it is hard to sleep at night.

Teacher: Well, make sure you sleep on the flight over. If you do not, you will be very tired.

Student: I have never been on a plane before, so I don t know if I will be able to sleep. Perhaps when it gets dark I will be able to sleep.

Teacher: Well, I hope you have a wonderful time at your new school. Please write to me and tell me what is happening in your life over there.

Student: I will write to you as often as I can.

Teacher: Good luck in your studies. If you have any difficulties, let me know and I will try to help you.

Student: Thank you for your kindness. I will keep that in mind.

Teacher: Good bye, have a safe trip.

Student: Thank you. I will see you next summer when I come home.

Teacher: Okay. We can sit and talk about your new life in America.

Chapter 2
Arriving and Settling in

到了，安顿下来吧

Guided Reading

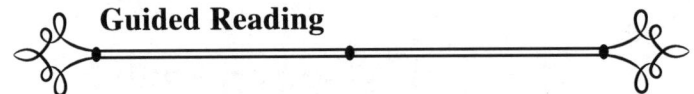

你知道坐国际航班要注意些什么吗?什么时间到机场合适,到了机场需要过哪些程序能保证你正常登机,坐上飞机后又要注意些什么,如何填写入境卡,如何过安检并安全取到你的行李?让我们来看看吧!

Before you read about arriving at the airport, let's talk about the airplane and what you need to do when you arrive at the airport in China. The first thing you need to remember when you are getting ready to travel abroad is to be at the airport early. The normal amount of time prior to departure is about 2 hours. The reason for this amount of time is that you can check in at the desk, get your boarding pass and go through the routine of checking your luggage in on time. Most people prefer to arrive at the airport three hours earlier since they feel that going through baggage check-in and security checks takes more time. It might be a good idea to be at the airport 3 hours before your flight.

When you get to the airport, go to the front counter of the airline you will be flying. If you are not sure where to go, simply ask around. There are people positioned all over the airport to help you find your way. Inside the main door of the airport terminal is an information desk. They can easily direct you to your check-in counter.

If you have never flown before, it is not as scary as you might think. If you are nervous about flying, ask for an aisle seat so you can't look out the window. Also, aisle seats are easier to get out of should you wish to use the bathroom. When you are at the check-in counter, your bags will be checked into the cargo hold of the plane except for the bag or two bags you can carry on the plane with you. The clerk will place a tag on each bag that you are checking in and give you a tab with numbers that match the tags on your bags. When you get to your destination you need to make sure you have the right bags and keep the tags with you. Someone might ask to see your tags and matching tabs. A general rule of caution: leave the tags on your bags until you get to your school or hotel.

When your flight is called for boarding, they usually have families with small children go on first. It is sometimes difficult to get the children settled. Then they call older people who might need assistance. After that, they have general boarding. Your bags must go in the overhead compartment. If you have a small bag, you can put it under the seat in front of you.

Sit down, fasten your seatbelt and enjoy the flight!

Before you arrive at your destination, the cabin crew will hand you a form to fill out for Customs. You must fill out the form completely because you will be handing it to a Customs Agent along with your passport when you arrive. Keep your passport, invitation from the school and your Customs form handy so you can get through the procedure quickly.

这儿有一份美国海关的出入境登记表，让我们一起试着填一填吧！

美国海关出入境登记表 (I-94 FORM) (中英文对照)	
U.S. Department of Justice OMR 1115-4077 Immigration and Naturalization service	美国司法部 OMR 1115-407 移民局
Welcome to the United State Admission Number **697385031 01**	欢迎来到美国 登记号码 (* 举例说明) 697385031 01
I-94 Arrival/Departure Record-Instructions	I-94 入境 / 离境记录说明
This form must be completed by all persons except U.S. citizens, returning resident aliens with immigrant visas, and Canadian Citizens visiting or in transit.	除了美国公民，美国海外侨民，和访问或过路的加拿大公民外，所有人士都必须填写此表。
Type or print legibly with pen in ALL CAPITAL LETTERS. Use English. Do not write on the back of this form.	请用大写字母打字或用钢笔或用圆珠笔清楚填写，请用英文填写，不要在此表背面填写任何东西。

This form is in two parts. Please complete both the Arrival Record (Item 1 through 13) and the Departure Record (Item 14 through 17).	此表包括两部分，请填写入境记录（第1项至第13项）和离境记录（第14项至第17项）两部分。
When all items are completed, present this form to the U.S. Immigration and Naturalization Service Inspector.	填写完毕后，请将此表交给美国移民局官员。
Item 7 – If you are entering the United States by land, enter LAND in this space. If you are entering the United States by ship, enter SEA in this space.	第7项内容说明□□□□□如果你从陆地进入美国，请在空格内填写LAND，如果你乘船进入美国，请在空格内填写SEA。
Form I-94(10-01-85)N	I-94 表 (10-01-85)N
Admission Number	登记号码
697385031 01	**697385031 01**
Immigration and Naturalization Service	移民局
I-94 **Arrival Record**	**I-94** 入境记录
1. Family Name	1. 姓
2. First (Given) Name	2. 名
3. Birth Date(Day/Mo/Yr)	3. 生日（月／日／年）
4. Country of Citizenship	4. 哪个国家公民
5. Sex (Male or Female)	5. 性别（男填MALE 或女填FEMALE）
6. Passport Number	6. 护照号码
7. Airline & Flight Number	7. 航空公司和航班号
8. Country Where You Live	8. 你在哪个国家生活
9. City Where You Boarded	9. 你在那个城市降落
10. City Where Visa Was Issued	10. 在哪个城市得到签证
11. Date Issued (Day/Mo/Yr)	11. 得到签证的日期（日／月／年）
12. Address While in the United State (Number and Street)	12. 在美国的住址（门牌号及街名）
13. City and State	13. 在美国的住址（市名及州名）
Departure Number	离境号码
697385031 01	**697385031 01**
Immigration and Naturalization Service	移民局
I-94 **Departure Record**	**I-94** 离境记录
14. Family Name	14. 姓

15. First (Given) Name	15. 名
16. Birth Date(Day/Mo/Yr)	16. 生日（日／月／年）
17. County of Citizenship	17. 哪个国家公民

美国海关申报／Custom Declaration Form（中英文对照）	
WELCOME TO THE UNITED STATES	欢迎来到美国
DEPARTMENT OF THE TREASURY UNITED STATES CUSTOMS SERVICE	财政部 美国海关署
CUSTOM DECLARATION	海关申报
1. Name: Last First　Middle　Initial	1. 姓名： 姓　　名　　中间名（首字线）
2. Number of family members traveling with you	2. 与你同行的家庭成员人数：
3. Date of Birth:　　　Month　Day　Year	3. 出生日期：　　　月　日　年
4. Airline/Flight:	4. 航空公司／航班号：
5. U.S. Address:	5. 在美居住地址：
6. I am a U.S. Citizen　　YES　NO If No, Country:	6. 你是一个美国公民吗　　是 否 如果不是，你是那个国家的公民：
7. I reside permanently in the U.S. YES NO If No, Expected Length of Stay:	7. 你是在美国永久居留吗　　是 否 如果不是，预期停留多久：
8. The purpose of my trip is or was **BUSINESS PLEASURE**	8. 此次旅程的目的是 商务旅游
9. I am/we are bringing fruits, plants,meats, food, soil, birds, snails, otherlive animals, farm products, or I/we have been on a farm or ranch outside the U.S.	Y E S NO	9. 你携带水果，植物，肉类，食品，土壤，鸟类，蜗牛，其他动物和农产品，或你一直居住在美国以外的农村或牧场吗	是 否
10. I am/we are carrying currency ormonetary instruments over $10000 U.S. or the foreign equiralent.	Y E S NO	10. 你携带现金或珍贵物品，其价值超过一万美金或相当于一万美金的外币吗	是 否
11. The total value of all goods I/we purchased or acquired abroad and am/are bringing to the U.S. is (see instructions under Merchandise on reverse side; visitors should report value of gifts only):$_____ U.S. Dollars	11. 你境外购买或获得并带入美国所有物品总价值（参看背面商品栏目；访问者只须申报礼品价值):$ ___ 美元
SIGN ON RESERSE SIDE AFTER YOU READ WARNING.(Do not write below this line.)	在你阅读警告之后请在背面签字（不要在此线下面签字）
INSPECTOR'S NAME STAMP AREA	检察员姓名　盖章区域
BADGE NO.	徽章号码

If you are going to the U.S., you might encounter a few unpleasant things when you arrive. Security check is not a great experience. If they ask you to choose either a pat-down or full body scan, the choice is yours. Here is the difference: A pat-down means that the security guard pats down your body as you stand with your arms raised. The full body scan is a screen you walk behind and it scans your entire body. A security guard sits and watches all full body scans looking for hidden weapons or drugs. The full body scan is faster if you are in a hurry to get out of the airport. Whichever one you choose, you will still have a lengthy wait to get through the process.

After you have been searched and your papers are in order, you can go and pick up your bags at the baggage claim area. Match the tabs you have with the tags on the bags and off you go. If you are asked to show a security guard your tabs and bags, just do so. Most of the time they will not ask to see the tags.

You are almost through the terminal. Now you move on to the arrival hall. This is where you will meet the people from your school who have come to help you. Look for a sign with your name on it, roughly about the size of A4 paper. If you see it, smile and wave. They will do the same.

Questions:

How was your flight?
How was the food?
Did they show a movie? What was the name of the movie?
Did you get to chat with anyone sitting near you?
Were you nervous on the flight?
How long was the flight?

Are you tired? Are you hungry?
Are you ready to go?

Depending on the time of day, you might be able to see a lot of the country or city as you travel to the school. Ask questions about what you have seen and your new-found friends will gladly answer them for you.

到了你求学的学校了，如何熟悉你的环境，如何交学费和取得经济上的援助，如何买到你的教材，到哪儿吃饭，宿舍的情况怎么样，好好安顿下来了！我们都将在这章里得到了解！

Upon arriving at the school, you will have many things to do. The person helping you will give you time to unpack your luggage and get acquainted with your roommate(s) and surroundings. They will tell you that they will be back to get you in one hour or two, so you will have a few moments to unwind and breathe.

Your helper, who will eventually become one of your friends, is probably in the same department as you, meaning that you will both be studying the same subjects. When they come to get you they will take you on a tour of the campus.

You will see the main buildings that you need to know: library, admissions office, dining hall, gymnasium, classrooms and bookstore. The other buildings you will become familiar with once you are on campus longer. So where do you go first?

The first stop for any new student is admissions. In the admissions building you will find out what classes you are taking, pay your tuition and find out about scholarships and financial aid. Whatever your major is, the department you are in there will also be information about scholarships. All you need to do is to ask the department secretary and he/she will help you. If you wish to be considered for a scholarship or financial aid, all of your paperwork must go through admissions and then on to financial services department.

After you have paid your tuition and found out which classes you will be taking, you and your new friends will end up at the bookstore. In the bookstore you can purchase new or used books for the classes you are taking. A suggestion about books is: If your class is a basic class, you might want to buy a used book. It is cheaper and most of the information you will use in class has already been outlined or highlighted by the previous owner(s). If the class is a special class, you might wish to buy a new book and keep it as a reference after you have completed your education. Either way, if you keep your books in good condition you can always sell them back to the bookstore and get some money in return.

Are you getting hungry? Well, now that you have an armload of books, it's time to hit the dining hall. Most schools have an all-you-can-eat dining hall. Part of your tuition is for food and at some point during the application process, you were asked to choose a meal plan. Most students choose a regular plan which means you will have 3 meals a day and you will have ample time to sit and enjoy your meal in between classes. Your friend will show you around the dining hall and how it works. It's not difficult to understand, however, all schools have their own way of setting up a dining hall depending on the number of students they must feed.

Now that you have finished your meal, it's time to go back to the dorm room and drop the books. Usually, the Resident Advisor (RA) will plan a party for all new students. This is called a "mixer". As a new student you will meet other students just like you. You will get to know them and the nice part is that they live in your building so new friendships will begin to bloom. At the

mixer you will hear about the rules of the dorm and meet some of the returning students. This is also the time when the RA tells students what activities are planned for the upcoming year. The students will elect representatives to speak for the dorm when the Student Union has meetings. If you have a complaint about the dorm, you can tell your representative and he/she will mention it at the next student union meeting.

So far, so good. After the mixer, students will either sit around and chat with each other or go back to their rooms and finish unpacking. Many students will take a look at the books they've purchased and start to worry about classes. Depending on the day of your arrival, classes will begin within a week's time. If you have any questions, go and ask your RA. His/her job is to make sure you are happy and that if you have any problems they will be handled quickly. The RA is employed by the school. Most RAs are graduate students at the school. They get free housing for helping the students.

You should be able to slow down for a bit and relax. It's always a good time to take a short nap after such a long flight' or you can roam the campus and see where everything is. Your choice.

Vocabulary

boarding pass 登机牌
security checks 安检
aisle [ail] n. 侧廊，（席位间的）通道
seatbelt [si:tbelt] n. 安全带
destination [ˌdestiˈneiʃən] n. 目的地，终点
cabin crew 乘务员
Customs [ˈkʌstəmz] n. 海关

encounter [in'kauntə] v. 遭遇，遇到，偶然碰到
pat-down n. 搜身
scan [skæn]n. 扫描，浏览，细看
weapon ['wepən] n. 武器，兵器
baggage claim 行李领取处
terminal ['tə:minl]n. 末端，终点站，终点
acquainted [ə'kweintid] adj. 熟悉的，认识的，了解的
unwind [ʌn'waind] v. 解开，松开，放松
gymnasium[dʒim'neiziəm] n. 体育馆，健身房
tuition[tju:'iʃən] n. 学费
scholarship ['skɔləʃip] n. 奖学金，学问，学识
financial aid [fai'nænʃəl] 经济援助
armload ['ɑ:mləud] n. 一抱之量
ample ['æmpl, 'æmpəl] adj. 丰富的，宽敞的，充足的
Resident Advisor 住宿顾问
bloom [blu:m] v. 开花，繁盛
complaint [kəm'pleint] n. 抱怨，疾病，诉苦，控告，投诉
purchase ['pə:tʃəs] vt. 购买
nap [næp] 打盹
roam [rəum] v. 漫游，闲逛，徜徉

Conversation Questions

What would be the first thing you would do when you arrive at the school?

Would you be more tired or excited?

What do you think the dorm room will look like?

Do you think you will be nervous when you arrive?

Will you change anything about yourself when you leave China? If so, what will you change?

Discussion Questions

How difficult will it be for you to leave your family and home to study abroad?

What is the one thing that you will miss about home?

Do you think your time at another school will be successful?

What do you think is the most difficult challenge ahead for anyone going abroad?

Do you think you will have second thoughts about going to another country? If yes, why? What kind of thoughts will you have?

Practice Dialogues

Throughout this book you will have a variety of dialogues that you can use to practice speaking and asking questions. Each section of the book will have 3 dialogues for your use.

Dialogue # 1 – Student and Customs Agent

Customs Agent: Next please. Please step up to the line.

Student: Okay. What do you want me to do?

Customs Agent: Please hand me your passport and the form you filled out on the airplane.

Student: Okay. Here are my papers.

Customs Agent: So, what country are you from?

Student: I am from China.

Customs Agent: And what brings you to the United States?

Student: I am here to study at the university.

Customs Agent: Did you bring any items with you that might be harmful? Such as food items or plants?

Student: No. Just my clothes and my computer for school.

Customs Agent: Okay, now I need you to go to the next area and you will be searched.

Student: Okay. Thank you for your help.

Customs Agent 2: Full body scan or strip search, which one would you prefer?

Student: I do not know.

Customs Agent 2: The full body scan is faster if you are in a hurry.

Student: Okay, let's do that one.

Customs Agent 2: Right. Walk through the area ahead and the machine will scan your body.

Student: Okay, thank you.

Customs Agent 2: Not at all.

Dialogue #2 – Meeting at the Airport

Susan: Hi, my name is Susan. I am from the university and I've come to pick you up.

Student: Hello. My name is _____. Very nice to meet you Susan.

Susan: I see you have your bags. Is there anything else we need to get for you before we leave the airport?

Student: No, I went through Customs, the scanning have got all my luggage. I am ready to go.

Susan: Great! Let's get out of here.

Student: Where are we heading now?

Susan: Well, first we will go back to the university. Once we get there, you will have some time to unpack and relax. I have a short meeting to attend and then we will take a tour of the campus.

Student: Sounds good to me.

Susan: Are you hungry?

Student: Not really. I ate on the plane. We had enough food because it was a long flight.

Susan: How long was your flight?

Student: I left Shanghai yesterday, so it took about 14 hours altogether.

Susan: Wow, you must really be tired now.

Student: I am tired, but I am also excited about being in America.

Susan: Most new students feel the same way. I hope you like here.

Student: Me too. I think it will be fun and exciting.

Susan: Well, it will take us about 1 hour to get to the university, so sit back and relax. It's a nice sunny day so you can see a lot of the city as we drive through it.

Student: I think I will take some pictures on the way to send back home to my parents.

Susan: Good idea. You can show them that you have arrived safe and sound.

Student: Yes.

Dialogue #3 – Student and Resident Advisor

RA: Hi, you must be _____ from China?

Student: Yes, I am.

RA: Well, my name is Jessica. I am the Resident Advisor for this building. You can call me Jessica. I am also a student here. I am working on my Masters in Child Psychology.

Student: Hello Jessica. My name is _____. I will be studying _____ here at the university.

RA: Well, let me show you to your room and tell you a bit about the dormitory and what goes on around here.

Student: Okay. Thank you.

RA: Here is your room. You have one roommate. You've already met her. Her name is Susan. She picked you up at the airport. Susan is in a meeting right now but will be back to take you on a tour in about 2 hours.

Student: Good. So we have 2 beds, 2 desks, 2 computers and our own bathroom?

RA: Yes. This is typical housing at the university. We also have a few students living alone.

Student: Wow. In China we have 6 to 8 students sharing a room half this size.

RA: That is crazy. There are some universities that put 4 students in a room, but the rooms are not small. It's like a bedroom with a living room and study room. So there is plenty of space for 4 students.

Student: Can you tell me where I can do my laundry?

RA: Sure. Downstairs in the basement we have several washing machines and dryers. When you need to use one ask Susan. She can show

you where they are located.

Student: Great. Thank you so much.

RA: A few rules for you. No loud music, no smoking or drinking in the dorm. We all like to have a quiet place to live, so if you want to listen to music just put on some headphones.

Student: Sounds good to me. Thanks Jessica.

Chapter 3
Orientation and Scheduling/ Choosing Classes

新生入学教育／
新生如何选课

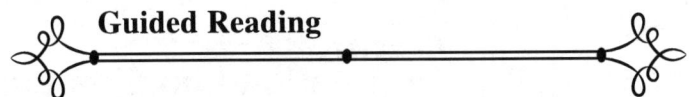

Guided Reading

　　进入八九月，国外大学的迎新活动陆续开始了，首次出国的新生们怀着不安的心情踏上异国的土地，迎接他们的将是什么呢？过来人告诉我们，其实不用担心，国外很多大学都有花样百出的迎新活动和入学教育，目的就是帮助新生尽快熟悉校园和同学，树立自信，更好地迎接即将到来的学习和生活！

Most new students to a college or university must attend orientation classes at the beginning of the semester. There are several reasons for this. Firstly, the school wants every student to understand that if they have any problems that there is always someone available to help. Secondly, the school expects students to behave as adults, not as children, and rules are set in place for that reason. Thirdly, many students coming to the school have never been away from home before and might feel lost. The orientation meeting is designed to build up self-confidence for each student.

As an international student, you will probably have a different orientation. Your orientation will be centered around the classroom. Actually, every class you take will begin with an orientation of the course by your teacher. Each teacher has his or her own specific rules for the class. Make sure you take good notes for each class during the first week of orientation. A few teachers might hand out a sheet of paper with their rules and requirements on it. If so, keep it.

Classroom orientation is the first thing that happens in the semester. The teacher tells you about themselves, offers some advice on how to pass their course and what they will and will not accept from their students. Tardiness is one example of what they will not accept. Being late to class is not a good idea and if you do it too many times, your teacher can fail you and you will have to make up the class. Some teachers will not allow eating in class. A drink is usually acceptable, but not food. The teacher will explain how he/she grades your assignments, homework, tests, etc. They might give you an e-mail address or telephone number so you can contact them, but almost all of them will tell you where their office is located and what office hours they keep for the semester.

Another form of orientation is by your peers. The people you are in class with or the people you live with in the dorm are your peers. As an international student, they will take you to various places so you can shop, eat, see the sights, etc. They will help you get settled in your college life and they will help you in getting around the city. As you do these things, try to keep a record of where you have been, how you get there and what you like or dislike about the place. You can always refer to these notes should you wish to venture out on your own and see the places again.

Some universities have employed students to show new students the campus and to assist them with banking, shopping and other tasks. These students are called 'work-study' students. They are hired as part of a financial aid package. They have jobs on campus to pay for part of their tuition.

In China, students move from class to class by the sound of a bell. The bell signals that class is about to begin and when class ends. In the US and most western countries, there is no bell system in the colleges and universities. Teachers let their students go when they finish class. Students have a schedule and they must follow it. As stated previously, being tardy for class is not a good idea. You are an adult and you should act like one. So, most students purchase alarm clocks or set their cellular phones for alarm so they can get up on time in the morning.

At any time if you do not understand what is being said at orientation, simply raise your hand and ask a question. People will not laugh at you nor will they hate you. They understand you are new and there are probably one or two other students wanting to ask the same question. Do not feel shy. Being shy in a western country will not help you. You need to stand up and be more self-confident. Teachers prefer it when students ask questions.

If students never ask questions, teachers would think they understand everything said and go on to the next topic. Never sit back and wait. Put your hand in the air and ask whatever you need to know.

For an international student coming to a western country for the first time, it would be a good idea to keep a small notebook with you at all times. You can jot down information about people, places, directions, phone numbers, etc. and use it as a quick reference. Many foreigners coming to China do the same thing. We jot down information, names of streets, restaurants, stores, etc. We also have students write down directions in Chinese for us so we can use the taxi when necessary. You should be able to do the same thing when you are in a western country. People will be very helpful by giving you the right information, they will not lie to you or get you lost.

What do you keep in this notebook? The first things you should record are your address at the school, your RAs phone number in case of emergency, your roommate's phone numbers and your own telephone number. Additional information would be your parents address and phone number, e-mail address if possible, and any information, medically, that a doctor would need to know. It is better to be safe than sorry.

伦敦政治学院有"迎新周"

在开学前两周，学校会给新生寄来新生手册，需要预备的各种物品清单也在其中。从新生如何入手创建自己的社团，到如何应对紧张情绪和压力，手册中事无巨细均有详细列明。"新生周"里，学校还会邀请家长参与迎新活动，游校园，与孩子的导师见面，各门选课老师汇聚一堂作自我推介。"迎新周绝对不是走个形式，做给学生和家长看，它的真正意义，是让我们用一种轻松、积极的心态，去迎接即将到来的全新大学生活

哈佛让新生感觉很自己很重要

哈佛的新生攻势全面而细致：让新生住进老生宿舍，让新生开派对；入学前几个月，邀请新生父母写一封信给哈佛本科学院院长，介绍自己孩子的特点和家长的关注点，以帮助学院更好地服务于新生，如安排合适的室友。"新生周"全校围着新生转，让新生感觉"自己很重要"，为新生父母安排"父母周末"，参观孩子宿舍、选听孩子的一堂课、在学校食堂吃饭、参观校医院等。

法国大学：每人独享一间宿舍

法国学生非常独立，即使父母都有车，很多学生都是独自一人开着二手车或者坐火车，兴高采烈地去学校报到。法国的学校宿舍非常注重学生个人的隐私，每位住校的学生都独享一间宿舍。与中国"浩浩荡荡"的车队送新生报到的景象相比，法国大学新生入学低调很多。

由于法国大学多是以口述的方式授课，对于非母语的学生而言，记笔记是非常吃力的，建议留学生要和法国学生搞好关系，以便向他们借笔记，比如说可以赠送具有中国特色的小礼物给法国同学。

美国大学：通过定向越野认识校园

美国一些校园较大的学校会在新生入学时将新生分成若干小组，由上一届学生会组织学生在校园内做类似定向越野的活动，新生被要求寻找学校及学校周边的重要建筑物及重要生活场所。美国校方在新生正式开学前通常都会有迎新活动，有些学校只是新生欢迎会，由老师或学长为新生介绍学校情况以及比较基本的注意事项；部分学校的迎新活动会持续一两周；有的学校会举办一些试听课，甚至举办入学测试，方便学生了解课程教授范围及学习难度，便于学生日后选课，同时这些测试还有助于学校以后进行分班。

英国大学：有学生半夜起来跑"火警"

在约克大学，导师会带领新生参观约克城市，以介绍当地战争历史为主，俗称"Ghost Walk"。导师会带着新生在约克闲逛，偶尔会在一块石砖或一个修道院前停下，向学生介绍这里的战争历史。

据毕业于英国拉夫堡大学的一名中国学生介绍，刚到学校的第一个月里，就经历了好几次"火警"。某个凌晨,火警铃忽然响起,他从床上爬起来,只来得及穿一件外套,以最快的速度带上桌面上的护照和钱包就往外跑,宿舍里的学生都穿着睡衣,泰然自若地站在宿舍前的空地。宿舍管理员则在淡定地清点到场人数。他才知道原来这是一次演习,事先完全不知情,最慢到场的会被校方用邮件通报批评。演习过后校方会通过邮件详细说明遇到火警时的注意事项,可见,英国学校是非常注重学生的人身安全。

专家给新生的一些建议:

1. 上好第一节课,老师通常会介绍课程以及考试设置,需要阅读的书本和资料,以及布置课程作业;

2. 多参加 Welcome Party(欢迎派对);

3. 善用学校资源。学校会为每位新生注册一个电子邮箱,这个邮箱的用处很大,学生会、学院的各种公告都会通过邮件通知,及时关注邮箱可以把握学校的每一个资源,例如免费语言课程的开课时间等。

After you have completed your orientation you should look at the courses being offered for the semester. Usually, all the courses are listed in a newspaper publication put out by the school several weeks before classes begin. Each school has a different method for listing classes, so if it looks confusing to you ask a roommate or your RA for help. They can explain it to you easily. Some universities go through course selection with new students during orientation. If so, make sure you ask questions about the courses before you sign up for them. What kind of question should you ask when choosing classes is up to you. Here are some of the normal questions that new students ask when they first start school:

1.Is the teacher easy or difficult?

2.Does the teacher give a lot of homework?

3.Is the teacher fun in class?

4. Will I learn a lot or will I be bored?

5. Is the teacher easy to talk to?

6. Can you understand what he/she is saying?

Another part of the course selection process is setting up your schedule. Again, every school has their own way of setting up class schedules, so be prepared to find some classes not available. Classes in western universities usually run on the following time schedule:

Monday – Wednesday – Friday = Each class is 45-50 minutes long.

Tuesday – Thursday = Each class is 75 – 90 minutes long.

So, knowing that a particular class only runs on Tuesdays and Thursdays, allows you to set up other classes on the remaining 3 days. If you choose a basic class, like English, you have a choice of taking the class 2 days a week (Tuesday/Thursday) or 3 days a week (Monday/Wednesday/Friday). The best way to approach course selection is to ask questions to students who have already taken classes, especially the classes you will be taking. They can give you information about the teacher, tests, homework, class time, and they might even be able to give you notes. You should be able to trust the other students and the RA to tell you about the teachers, courses and other information. They will not lie to you.

When choosing your classes, the nice part is that the schedule is quite flexible. If you want to sleep during the week, you can set up a schedule where your classes begin later in the day. If you are a morning person, you can set up early classes and have the afternoons free. If you want to challenge yourself and have a lot of extra free time, set up your schedule so that your classes are on Tuesdays and Thursdays only. That gives you 5 days free to do homework, explore the city or sleep. Beware though, Tuesday/Thursday classes are a little longer, but they also require you to do more homework. Once you learn how to set up your schedule, the next semester will be easier for you.

A few notes about class schedules:

1. Some classes get filled up very quickly and the teacher issues a notice closing the class. This means you have to find another class to take.

2. Some schools will close classes if there are not enough students signed up for the class. If this is the case, you can't change it. You are out of luck and must find another time to take the class.

3. Most of the basic classes: English, Math, Physical Education, Biology, etc., will list at least 10 classes each and sometimes up to 30 or 40. All have different days where they are held, starting times, etc. So you have lots of classes to choose from.

4. You might need a class that is closed, and if so, you need to meet with the professor and ask to be added to the class roster. If you explain why you need the class, the professor will make a decision. Sometimes they are good about making such decisions, sometimes they are not. If you can't get into the class you want because it is closed, try to find another class that will fit your schedule.

5. Usually International students take about 15 credits the first semester. This means you will be taking 5 – 3 credit classes. Every school has a list of required classes that students must take as part of their degree program. If you look in the student handbook, you will see your program spelled out in detail for your major. Simply follow the schedule and you will be fine.

6. If you could choose a class and find out that the teacher is too difficult to understand, you can usually change the class within the first two weeks of classes. The information about the add/drop rules for schedule changes is listed inside the course selection guide.

让学生提前了解各种课程的"信息大餐"

让新生提前了解大学提供的各类课程的"信息大餐",是学校帮助新生"打有准备之仗"的选课策略之一。新生报到后,学校就会为他们提供一本"选课手册",手册对选课注意事项和学校提供哪些课程进行讲解与介绍。

学校在向新生介绍各门课程时也动了点"小脑筋",不仅尽量避免语言枯燥,有时还提出一些可探讨的话题,利用学生的好奇心激发他们对这门课的兴趣。学校这样做的目的是要让即使完全没有相关知识储备的新生,也能了解课程主要传授哪方面的知识。此外,学校还会列出课程的参考书目,让新生从中了解将来要扩展的知识面以及可能承受的课程压力,这样,他们选课时就能更加明确这门课的整体学科方向。

大学教授有问必答

美国的一些大学在"迎新周"上会举行院系宣展会。每个系都由几名教授坐镇,守住各自的"展台",派发课程手册和传单,宣传本院系开设的课程。有些院系的展台上还会摆出一架游轮模型或几个昆虫标本吸引学生参观。教授们热情洋溢地介绍本系的课程和研究成果,耐心解答新生们的问东问西,然后化身"有问必答哥"。如果这还不足以让新生全面了解各门课程的话,他们还可以到院系办公室索取查看每门课程整个学期的上课计划进度表(Syllabus),上面详尽列出课程目标、每次上课进度、评分标准以及书单等项目,有些学校也为学生提供在线查询此类信息的平台。这些都为新生选课提供了实际的参考。

学业导师帮助选择适合课程

美国大学的新生通常在入校伊始就会配有一名学业导师。学业导师的选派往往是根据新生入学申请表上的专业志愿选定的。新生选课前会与学业导师进行一次沟通,讲述自己的兴趣喜好、知识背景、学术能力以及选课计划等。学业导师会根据每位新生的不同情况,同时考虑他的学业规划和个人成长,给出更有针对性的个性化建议,帮助新生选择目前最适合自己的课程,减少选课的盲目性。如果在开学一周内学生感到所选课程并不适合自己，也可以及时联系导师进行调整。

学业导师通常不会建议新生在入校伊始就过早地限制了自己的选课和学业计划，而是鼓励他们多体验一些不同的东西，尝试挑战不同的学科。勇敢地在未知领域"探险"，进行多元化学习才能更加了解自己和世界，这也是大学提倡的"淘课"精神所在。

除此之外，一些学校还会安排新生家长与学业导师见面交流，讨论孩子的学习计划。有的大学欢迎家长选听孩子的一堂课，亲身体会课堂氛围等。学校希望家长可以更明白学校的开课特点，再结合自己孩子的条件，从家长的角度向孩子提出学业上的建议。

学长评价有助于正确选课

不过，学业导师提出的毕竟只是建议，学生最终决定选修哪些课程，还得自己拿主意。为了方便学生选课，不少学校都制作了专门的选课网站。学生不仅可以在上面快速勾选要选的课程，也可以在每门课程的介绍下面看到曾经选修过该课的学生评价，据此再次判断这门课程和授课的老师是否与自己的要求相符。比如，当一门课程被评价为"课程内容很好，可惜教授的印度口音太严重"时，对此介怀的学生可能就望而却步了；如果有的学生不喜欢讲课无聊的老师，也许他就不会选择去听一位性格古板的教授讲一些令他昏昏欲睡的内容；如果有学生发现他一学期选择的10门课中有6门被评价为"课业繁重"，那他就要考虑是否要把其中的两门课挪到下个学期再修，以便更合理地安排自己的学习时间。

After you have registered for classes and the Registrar's Office has given you a printed version of your schedule, you need to head to the Campus Bookstore to buy your books. When you enter the bookstore you will find all kinds of textbooks. Do not panic. If you need help, just ask. The schedule that you have in your hands is the most useful item you need when you are in the bookstore. Each class has a specific course number

that identifies it. All textbooks are set up according to the subjects. For example, you need to take English 101, a basic English class for first year students. When you look at the English books there will be a sign in front of the English books, and the one you need will show: ENG101 on it. Now, you know what book to buy, but is it the right one? Perhaps. To be sure, you need to look at the card again and see what teacher is listed on the card. Each teacher can choose any book they wish for their classes. However, basic classes like English are considerably large and many students must take them. So the books in the basic classes are used by all the teachers. As you go through your years at the school, you will find specific books which have been chosen by some of your teachers. Remember to check the card on the shelf for the following information:

1. Course Name and Course Number

2. Professor's name who is teaching the course

3. Day and Time of the class which is scheduled

The information on the card should match the information on your schedule. Once you've checked everything, pick up the book and continue your shopping. If at any time you need help just ask someone. There will be many people in the bookstore to help new students. In some schools, someone from the orientation meeting will help you get your books. It all depends on the school you go to and how they organize such things.

A few notes about textbooks:

1. You can choose to buy a new book at full price or buy a used book at a lower price. If you choose to buy a new book, put your name in it in case you leave it somewhere and it will be returned to you.

2. Used books are a good bargain, especially if you are worried about money. However, know that once you buy a new book and put your name

in it, you lose almost 50% of the price if you decide to sell it back to the bookstore.

3. You can also look around campus for bulletin boards where students post cards trying to sell old textbooks that they no longer need. Some students will even give you the notes for the class if you buy the book from them. It's your choice.

4. At the end of each semester, some of your books will not be used again. English 101 textbooks are usually used for the entire first year, so you need to keep them. If you do not want the books any longer, you can sell them by posting a card on the bulletin boards around campus or by selling them back to the Campus Bookstore. They will give you some money, but not much. A hint about selling books back to the Campus Bookstore, try not to mark in the book. If you do not mark in the book you will get more money back.

Vocabulary

orientation [ˌɔ:rien'teiʃən] n. 方向，定位，取向，排列方向；任职培训；
behave [bi'heiv] v. 行为，举止
self-confidence ['self'kɔnfidəns] n. 自信
peers [piəz] n. 同伴，同事
venture ['ventʃə, 'ventʃə(r)] v. 敢于，冒险
work-study ['wə:kˌstʌdi] n. 勤工俭学
signal ['signəl] v. 标志，用信号通知
tardy ['tɑ:di:] adj. 迟到的，迟缓的
jot [dʒɔt] v. 略记，摘要记载下来
tardiness ['tɑ:dinəs] n. 缓慢；迟延；拖拉

record ['rekɔ:d] n. 记录，记载；档案，履历；唱片；最高纪录

refer [ri'fə:] vt.& vi. 参考，查阅

requirements [ri'kwaiəmənt] n. 要求；必要条件；必需品，需要量；资格

disliked [dis'laikt] v. 不喜欢，厌恶 (dislike 的过去式和过去分词)

banking ['bæŋkiŋ] v. 堆积 (bank 的现在分词)；筑（堤）；将（钱）存入银行；

self-confident [self'kɔnfidənt] adj. 自信的，自持的

medically ['medikli] adv. 医学上地，医药上地； 体格上地

quick reference [kwik 'refrəns] 快速参考

prefer[pri'fə:] vt. 更喜欢； 提升，提拔； vi. 更喜欢，宁愿

newspaper ['nju:s,peipə] n. 报纸，报； 旧报纸； 新闻纸

morning person ['mɔ:niŋ 'pə:sən] n. 喜欢早起的人

publication [,pʌbli'keiʃən] n. 出版； 出版物； 公布； 发表

flexible ['fleksəbl] adj. 灵活的； 易弯曲的； 柔韧的； 易被说服的

method ['meθəd] n. 方法； 条理

confusing [kən'fju:ziŋ]adj. 令人困惑的； 混乱的； 混淆的

afternoons [,a:ftə'nu:nz] adv. 每天下午 ; n. 下午 (afternoon 的名词复数)

Campus Bookstore ['kæmpəs 'bʊk,stɔ:, -,stəʊr] 校园书店

difficult ['difikəlt] adj. 困难的；难做的；难解的；不易相处的

challenge ['tʃælindʒ] vt. 质疑；向…挑战 vi. 提出挑战，要求竞赛（或竞争）；驳斥

Registrar's Office ['redʒi,stra:z 'ɔfis] n. 注册办公室

registered ['redʒistəd] adj. 注册的；登记过的；已挂号的；v. 记录；登记；注册

issues ['isju:z] n.（特别重要或大众关注的）问题 v. 发表；宣布；分配

bored [bɔ:d] adj. 无聊的，无趣的，烦人的 v. 令人厌烦 (bore 的过去式和过去分词)；挖

roster ['rɔstə, 'rɔ:stə] n. 花名册；勤务簿；登记簿

credits ['kredits] n. 存款；学分

decision [di'siʒən] n. 决定；果断；决议

handbook ['hændbuk] n. 手册；指南

version ['və:ʃən] n. 版本；译文，译本；说法

spelled out [speld aut] 拼出，读出；阐明

add [æd] vt. 增加；补充； 附带说明；把…包括在内

drop [drɔp] vt.& vi. （使）落下；投下；（使）降低；减少

panic ['pænik] vi. 十分惊慌 adj. 恐慌的，惊慌失措的

specific [spi'sifik] adj. 明确的；特种的；具体的

identifies [ai'dentifaiz] v. 认出 (identify 的第三人称单数)；支持；确认；辨认

according [ə'kɔ:diŋ] adv. 依照

considerably [kən'sidərəbli] adv. 相当，非常，颇

bargain ['bɑ:gin] n. 特价商品；便宜货 vt. 做交易 vi. 讨价还价；达成协议

bulletin boards ['bulitin bɔ:d] n. （电子）公告牌

posting ['pəustiŋ] v. 邮寄；张贴 (post 的现在分词)；公布

Conversation Questions

If someone asked for directions, would you help them?

Do you tend to get lost when you are in a new place?

How can you keep from getting lost in a new country?

What would you carry with you at all times?

Will you spend time alone or with friends?

Will you spend much time in the library?

What will be the most difficult thing for you when you start your classes?

What will you do if you encount a problem?

Do you think it will be easy for you to make new friends?

What would be a good time to go to sleep at night?

Discussion Questions

Do you think orientation is useful for new students?

What was orientation like for you at your school in China?

What kind of questions would you ask a teacher the first day of class?

Can you think of any other information to put in the notebook?

Do you take good notes or are you lazy about it?

Practice Dialogues

Throughout this book you will have a variety of dialogues that you can use to practice speaking and asking questions. Each section of the book will have 3 dialogues for your use.

Dialogue # 1 – 2 Students

A: Hi, what's your name?

B: My name is _____.

A: So, where are you from?

B: I'm from China.

A: How long have you been in the US?

B: Just for a few days now.

A: Any thoughts about our country? The people? The school?

B: I haven't had much time to sit and think about everything. Orientation is moving quickly.

A: I know what you mean. My name is Sasha. I'm from Russia.

B: Nice to meet you Sasha. How long have you been here?

A: Oh, I arrived last week.

B: Do you like it here?

A: Oh yes. The school is really large and the other students have been very kind and helpful to me.

B: Well that's good to know. I hope we can become good friends this year.

A: I think we will. Say, what classes are you taking this semester?

B: I'm not sure yet. I think I have to take the basic classes like everyone else.

A: Well we should register for the same classes and then we can study together.

B: That sounds like a good idea. They told me that I should find other people to study with since we do not study in groups back in China.

A: The only way to get through the courses is to study in a group. You can use others opinions to help you figure things out.

B: Sounds good to me. Let's go register when the orientation is over.

A: Okay.

Dialogue #2 – Student with Registration Official

Student: Excuse me. I need to register for classes.

R.O.: Okay. Do you have your student ID with you?

Student: Yes, here it is.

R.O.: Good. Now, since you are a new student and this is your first year, you need to take at least 15 credits of classes. You can take up to 18 if you wish. Any number of credits higher than 18 would have to be approved by the head of the department for your major. Do you understand?

Student: I think so. If not, I will ask as we go along.

R.O.: That's a good idea.

Student: So all I have to do is follow the guidelines for my major and take the basic classes that the department has outlined in the student handbook?

R.O. Yes and no. You need to take the basic classes for the first 2 years. Afterwards, you concentrate on your major for the final 2 years. When you choose the basic courses you want, you also must take some electives. The electives can be anything that is of interest to you. However, you might want to choose courses that would help you in your major. Like computers.

Student: Oh, I see. Yes, a computer class would be useful since I will be doing a lot of writing this year. Thanks for the information.

R.O.: Not at all. Just come back if you have any problems or questions.

Student: Okay, thanks again. Bye.

R.O.: Bye.

Dialogue #3 – Student in the Bookstore

Clerk: Okay, who is next?

Student: That would be me.

Clerk: Let me see your class schedule and student ID, please.

Student: Here you go.

Clerk: So, you are a freshman and you are majoring in Business.

Student: That's right.

Clerk: See that sign hanging from the ceiling over there? That is the Business area. All your textbooks for Business will be there. But first, you need to get your basic classes out of the way.

Student: Tell me where I should go first.

Clerk: Start at the top of your schedule and work your way down. Looks like English is the first one and those books are over there on your left. Just look at the signs hanging from the ceiling. Go to each section you need and if you can't find what you need, ask the person working in that section. They will help you out.

Student: Okay. English first on the left, then on to the other sections. So, Business is last on my list?

Clerk: It is your major and you will have only introductory classes in Business for the first 2 years. You only need a few books from that section now. Eventually all your books will be from that section.

Student: Got it. Thanks for your help.

Clerk: No problem. Good luck with your classes.

Student: Thanks.

Chapter 4
Getting around the Campus
熟悉校园

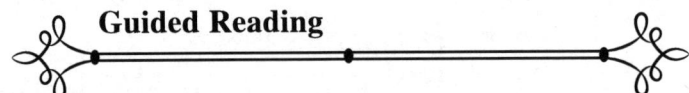

Guided Reading

来到新的环境,碰到陌生的面孔,遇到新的挑战,一切都不一样了。忐忑不安的你该如何去适应新的环境,如何去安排自己的生活和学习? 不要急,这章能给你所需要的指导和答案,快来看看吧!

New students on a campus go through a range of emotions when they first arrive. They are excited, happy, nervous, frightened and anxious. As they grow accustomed to their new surroundings, they begin to relax and set up a routine. However, the first few weeks of classes can still be scary and nerve-wracking for anyone. As an international student, how do you ease these fears? Well, you have already met a few people and they have become your new friends. You have had a tour of the campus so you know where everything you might need is located. One thing you can do to get rid of the nerves, especially during the first few weeks of classes, is to plan your day ahead of time. Before going to bed at night, sit down and make a list of what you must do the next day. If you have to write down every little thing, then do it. The key to getting rid of the nerves you are feeling is allowing yourself enough time to get where you need to go.

We are all nervous the first few weeks of class. It is more than just nerves, though. It's the excitement of being in a new environment, meeting new people, teachers and facing the challenges that university life has to offer. So as you prepare your list, think of all the things you need to do and give yourself time to do them. For example, get up and take a shower…eat breakfast…get to my first class at 8:00am…go to my second glass at 9:15am…have lunch at noon…go to the library from 1:00 until 3:00…meet my friends in the dining hall…etc. Most new students will get up an hour earlier so they can get their day started. After a few weeks of this, you will settle into a routine and sleep a little later in the morning. Just remember, the key is time and giving yourself enough time to get where you need to be.

In China, students tend to decide for themselves if classes or even certain topics are worth their time. If they feel they can spend their time doing something else that is more enjoyable or more beneficial, they will

skip classes. Unfortunately, this mindset will not be tolerated in western countries. Being late or absent is not something you want to do. There is no special treatment for international students, so never think that you will be given a second opportunity if you miss a class or two. When you come to the university you are an adult and you have many responsibilities. If you are late, call someone. If you are ill, call someone and ask a classmate to take notes for you. You might even consider sending an email to the teacher letting them know you will not be in class and that you will get the notes from a classmate. Even scheduling an appointment with the teacher would help you to catch up on what you missed. At the end of the day, it is all up to you.

If you keep a notebook you can find out when various buildings on campus are opened or closed. The main buildings you need to know about are the clinic, the dining hall, the library, the bookstore and your dormitory. So look for signs that tell you the hours of operation. Jot them down in your notebook so you can refer to them when needed.

Many international students feel the need to buy a used car when they arrive at the school so that they can travel around without having to ask others for a ride. The only problem you would face is your driver's license. You would have to get a license for the country you are in or have an international driver's license that the host country would accept. Once that hurdle is cleared, one of your friends could accompany you to look at cars. Another option, which also depends on where you are located, is getting a bicycle. Most universities have bicycle stands outside of major buildings. You put your bicycle in the stand and lock it. A word of caution about bicycles: Purchase a used one instead of a new one. A new one is more likely to be stolen and you would save yourself some money.

Perhaps the best thing about western universities is that they are communities where everyone gets along. If you are lost and need help, simply ask anyone near you. They will point you in the right direction. Every department, while separate, is still part of the community. Activities held in various departments are always open to the entire school. So, at any time that you feel lost just ask for help. It is not a problem.

高效的学习技巧

第一步 树立正确的学习目标

美国的一位心理学家曾经指出：如果一个铅球运动员在比赛的时候没有目标，那么，他的成绩一定不会很好。如果他心中有一个奋斗目标，铅球就会朝着那个目标飞行，而且投掷的距离就会更远。这个比喻非常形象，它具体地说明了学习目标的重要性。当我们有了一个追求的学习目标时，才会有不懈地努力，向着心中既定的目标前进。制定了学习目标，也就明白了学习的方向与学习的进度，而不是盲目的学习。所以任何一个学习者都要树立正确的学习目标，因为有了目标才会有学习的动力。

第二步 合理制订学习计划

合理的学习计划才能起到促进作用，过高和过低的学习计划都不能达到应有的效果。如何制定合理的学习计划呢？

首先，不能制订太高的学习计划。虽然较高的计划可以增强自己的学习积极性，但是，假设因为某些不可避免的原因，计划不能实现，那么势必对自己的信心造成影响，继而影响学习的积极性。

其次，也不能制定太低的学习计划。如果把学习计划定得太低，虽然很容易达到，但自己的动力却得不到充分的体现，同时也无法通过学习有效地提高自己的能力。此外还有可能助长自满和狂妄的情绪，总以为自己很聪明而不想付出更多的学习精力。

第三，学习计划不能定得太过于死板。一些学生把自己的学习计划制定得太死板，一切都按照条条框框进行，甚至出现哪一个小时学习哪门功课的情况。这样

的计划看起来很清楚、明白，但是太死板，死板的学习计划容易导致学习兴趣的降低。

第四，学习计划也不能定得太松。如果学习计划太"灵活"，在执行的时候又会觉得起不到计划的作用。所以，在制定时又不能过于笼统、松散，否则学习计划就形同虚设。

第五、计划要长短结合。学习是一门艺术，必须讲究和谐和内在的平衡。我们在制定学习计划的时候，要注意长期计划和短期计划的结合。长远计划可以确定学习方向，而短期计划则可以更好地落实学习内容。将二者有机地结合起来，才能更好地提高学习效率。

第三步 认真执行学习计划

1．订立"每天计划"：在订立长期计划的同时，我们必须订立"每天计划"，并严格按照计划实行。如果有一天因为特殊情况而耽误了学习，不应该随便就放弃当天的学习，一定要找空余时间弥补起来。也就是说，要把所有的计划落实到天。

2．"坚持"要贯穿计划中："坚持"是计划实施过程中最难的。在实施计划时，一时看不到进步不要心焦，更不要气馁、轻言放弃。学习计划一定要每天执行，而且贵在坚持，如果某一天的任务拖下了，就要及时补上去，否则学习账就会越欠越多，最终将整个学习计划拖垮。

3．计划要灵活：计划一定要灵活，即在执行时还要做到随时根据自己的学习时间，学习效果等相关的因素做出适当的调整。

第四步 合理安排学习时间

1．找到学习的黄金时间：对于学习效果来说，首先应该考虑学习方法的运用是否得当。不正确的学习方法，花的时间越多，学习效率就越低。除此以外，如果要更好地提高学习效率，就要找出自己比较适合学习的时间段，然后充分利用这段时间学习，可以达到事半功倍的效果。科学证明，人在刚吃饱饭时，头脑反应较迟钝，而在起床后的2－3小时，头脑最清晰、敏锐，因此如果我们善于把握这些规律，就可以提高学习效率；反之，则形成浪费。

2．合理利用空档时间：要提高学习效率，就必须充分利用空档时间。比如，老师提前了三分钟下课，或者放学回家在公共汽车站多等了20分钟等等。这些时间都称为空档时间。合理运用生活中的空档时间学习。这是一个提高学习效率最好的方法之一。

3. 好的心境可以节约读书时间：在面对某些不能马上解决的问题，而不能专心致志读书时，千万不能沮丧，要积极地想办法将那些问题解决。一旦调整好了心态，心情就会好起来，心也就会放在读书上了。在这里，重要的是遇到问题时千万不要拖延，要在适当的时机勇敢果断地做出解决。

第五步 提高听课效率

1. 思维要跟上：上课的时候，听课效率要高，听课的思维一定要跟着老师的思维路线走。如果思维一旦跟不上，就不能正确理解老师讲解的内容。特别是逻辑比较强的学习内容，思维的跟上显得更为重要。所以，在听课的时候要积极运用自己的思维能力，与老师的思维节奏紧密配合，听课的效率才会提高。

2. 抓住听课四要素：为了更好地发挥课堂上的自主性，我们必须明确在听课的时候要注意的三个要素。

1）眼到：所谓眼到就是听课的时候，将眼睛这个感觉器官的作用充分地发挥出来。但是眼睛的作用绝对不仅仅是盯着黑板而已。眼睛在课堂上的灵活运用要根据不同的内容而定。

2）口到：口到是指要加强朗读，随时发问。在课堂上一旦有疑难问题时，就需要及时发问，争取在课堂上把所有疑难问题弄清楚。有的学生或许是因为性格内向，即使遇到没有听懂的问题也不主动问老师，这不是很好的学习方法。

3）心到：老师在讲课的时候，只起个引导作用，最主要的还是靠自己思考。这就要求在听课的时候要注意心到。在课堂上时刻都要用心，这是听好课的基础。

On your first day of class, your teacher will tell you what he/she expects from you for the semester. Being punctual is on their list. They might have an established rule regarding lateness. Make sure you know it and understand it. Aside from being ill and in the clinic, there should be no reason for you to miss class.

Remember, until you get settled in to your class schedule; give yourself enough time to get around the campus. Your friends might think you are crazy for doing this, but it will help calm your nerves and clear your head. The newness of university life will quickly wear off, so make sure you know your way around the campus.

Clinic- (医务室)

One building you should become familiar with is the clinic. The clinic is run by a team of professionals. Usually there are 2 doctors and a few nurses to help you if you have problems. At some point during your orientation you need to set up an appointment with the clinic for a physical examination. The examination is routine and nothing to worry about. Students are given a physical exam to see if they are able to participate in physical education classes. The doctor will examine you. He/she will check your heart beat, your temperature, in some cases they will take you to the local hospital for a chest x-ray to make sure your lungs and heart are in good shape. They also test your reflexes by tapping on your kneecaps. Another part of the exam is blood work. The nurse will take 1-2 tubes of blood to check for any illnesses like diabetes, anemia, etc. Once you are finished with the examinetion you can attend physical education classes. If you have taken a medical physical prior to entering the U.S., for visa purposes, make sure you keep a copy of all the documents. You can give them to the doctor at the clinic and they will keep them in a file for you. Giving this information to the doctor might expedite your exam in the clinic.

The clinic is open every day but not 24 hours a day. If you are ill during the day, you can go to the clinic. If you are ill on the weekend, you might be able to go to the clinic or you will have to go to the local hospital. Either way, you will get the help you need. The main thing to remember when you go to the clinic is to have your student ID card with you. Your file in the clinic is set up according to your ID number. So keep it with you at all times.

Library- (图书馆)

Knowing the library location and hours will be very helpful. The library is one place where you will spend a lot of time while in the US. Many teachers at the university will set up class visits to the library so you can have a tour of the facilities. The teachers want you to be aware of what resources are available to you on campus. They don't want you to sit in front of a computer all day, so some of them will assign tasks that require you to explore the library in order to complete the tasks. It's a great way to learn about the library. As a freshman, you should give yourself some time to simply walk around the library and look. If you have questions, the librarian or library staff will help you. Just ask them. If they are not too busy, they will give you a tour of the library and answer questions as you walk around.

University libraries have various hours of operation. They also have various rules when it comes to checking out books. For example, you can check out up to 10 books but only for a 2 week period. If the books are brought back late, you have to pay a fine. The fine could be 5 cents a book for each day or more. Ask the librarian about fines for overdue books. Another part of the library that you will find out about as you go through your education is called the back stacks. The back stacks are periodicals and journals that are located in the back of the library, most of the time you can not see them in the library. They are in another room. The back stacks are used by graduate students and professors who are doing research. At some point you will be asked to do research and then you will be shown the back

stacks. The library, like the clinic requires that you bring your student ID with you. Some university libraries will not allow a student in the front door without a student ID. You can not check out a book without your ID.

Dining Hall- (食堂)

For most students the most important building to know is the campus dining hall. The dining hall opens early in the morning so students can get breakfast before they go off to classes. The method for paying for food is quite easy. You sign up for a food plan when you register at the beginning of the year. You must have your student ID with you when you go to the dining hall. You have a special microchip in your ID card that identifies what meal plan you have purchased for the year. The dining hall has a special machine that reads your ID card and it tells the cashier what plan you have and how many meals you have had daily.

Another option is to buy a meal card. This card works like a debit card. You put money on the card and purchase food through the card. If you wish you can also purchase items at the bookstore using the same card. The only thing you need to worry about it making sure you have enough money on your card to cover the cost of your purchases.

The dining hall is where you will meet your friends, sit and chat about classes and make plans for the weekends. It is one of the social areas on the university campus. It is also one of the places where new students gain weight. The 'freshmen fifteen' is a phenomenon that exists on every university campus in America. The idea is that new students coming to the university will be shocked by the amount of food available to them at breakfast, lunch and dinner. Most dining halls are buffet-style, meaning you can eat as much as you like. The only problem you face is how much weight will you gain? On the average, freshmen gain 15 pounds in their first year of school, hence the name 'freshmen fifteen' is born. If you can control your eating, you will be fine. However, there are some who have never seen such a variety of food and they simply go crazy. Can you imagine the following items all sitting there waiting for you!

fresh fruit	pies	ice cream	steak	chicken
salad	pizza	sodas	seafood	pasta
vegetables	breads	drinks	eggs	cereals
cookies	cakes	rice	milk	pancakes

And it is all you can eat. When you get to the university and you go to the dining hall, remember…. 'freshmen fifteen'. If you are not convinced, ask your RA or any returning student about it. They can tell you how much they gained or how they avoided gaining a lot of weight. All university students in the U.S. know about the 'freshmen fifteen'.

国外高校的食堂

美国大学： 食堂菜单学生做主

在美国科尔比学院，各个食堂每天供应的菜品不同，学生在学校网站的餐饮服务页面上可以轻松查到每个食堂当天的菜单。如果学生觉得某道菜的味道不敢恭维，或是吃得太久已经腻了，只要在卡片上或者电子邮件里写下对食堂的建议，餐饮服务部就会根据这些建议改良或增减菜品。

在美国康奈尔大学有三十多个校园食堂，总体营业时间从早上7点到次日凌晨2点，学生完全不必担心饿了却没有东西可吃。此外，校园里还流动着著名的食品卡车（提供披萨、三明治等）和周末推出的流动薄饼店，学生随时可以在这些"会走的食堂"里买到既饱腹又美味的食品。

为保证食材的新鲜，美国圣·奥拉夫学院食堂所需的原材料尽可能在当地购买——蔬菜、肉类都由该校学生经营的有机农场提供，确保肉类中不含抗生素和生

长激素；苹果来自一个距离学校只有几分钟路程的果园；乳制品则全部出自本市的一个家族农场。也许食材的绿色、健康、美味，正是该校食堂敢夸下海口说"几乎没人抱怨圣·奥拉夫食品"的信心来源。

韩国大学：有专门的宿舍食堂

韩国大学里有专门的宿舍食堂与对外食堂。宿舍食堂是不对外的，宿舍费用里边就包括了住宿和三餐的开销。中国很多的大学食堂，基本上属于半自助式的，有很多菜色，可以任由学生自己挑选，因为花样太多，学生们常常为自己要吃什么而烦恼。在韩国，却正好相反。很多宿舍食堂（包括学校里的对外食堂）基本上没有什么可以挑的，一个主菜，两个配菜，一个汤。想吃不想吃也就是这些。当然有的对外食堂，会有别的菜肴可供选择，可是相比中国国内大学的食堂来说，样式真的太少了。

建国大学是韩国著名的私立大学，总校位于韩国的首都首尔。建国大学的学生宿舍号称是全韩最漂亮和干净的。一楼有餐厅、洗衣房、面包店、邮局、便利店。宿舍的一楼是自助餐厅，学生一般会选择晚上吃，吃饭的时间比较充裕。

日本用数字"量化"健康

在拥有超过一百三十所大学的东京，"价廉"是所有大学食堂的特点。为了吸引学生前来就读，"物美"和"环境美"亦成为许多大学食堂发展的新方向。

学校食堂为学生提供的不仅有美味，还有"量化"的健康。日本北海道大学的中央食堂专门为想减肥和需要控制体重的学生提供一项服务，即这张小票上不仅有菜品、价格，还有菜品对应的卡路里，并在小票底部计算出这一餐饭摄入的卡路里总数。这对于想通过控制饮食保持身材的学生来说无疑是"福音"，不仅可以帮助学生保持身材，也可以帮助学生选择更为合理、健康的膳食。

英国大学："魔法"食堂座位按级别划分

喜爱《哈利·波特》系列电影的观众一定会对影片中霍格沃茨魔法学校那宏伟庄重、穹顶布满星星的大餐厅印象深刻。这个餐厅的原型就是世界著名学府英国牛津大学的基督学院食堂，也叫"大礼堂"。

基督学院始建于1524年，是牛津大学最大也是最古老的学院，基督学院食堂是这个学院最重要的组成部分，现在仍然作为学生食堂。令人羡慕的是，牛津大学的学子们可以每天在这个被波特迷视为圣地的地方用餐。教授们也仍保留着与学生共同进餐的传统。

食堂每天供应四餐，早餐、中餐，而晚餐则分两次。下午六点的晚餐是非正式的，学生和老师可以着便装用餐。而晚上八点半这一轮则是正式晚宴，来用餐的人必须穿着正式的服装。

食堂的座位也是按照级别划分的。比如餐厅的座位有"高桌"和普通座之分，只有教授、资深研究员或访问研究员等才能登上"高桌"，学生只能坐普通座位。

Gymnasium- （体育馆）

If you are an athlete, you will want to spend more time in the gymnasium. As you walk around the campus, learning where things are located, try to find the gym. Eventually you will have classes in the gym. However, if you want to keep in shape and have a workout, the gym usually has a schedule posted for students who want to use the facilities. You can run the track, lift weights in the weight room, go for a swim in the pool or play basketball, tennis, ping-pong or any other sport they offer. Most university campuses have other athletic facilities for students to use like: tennis courts, basketball courts, handball courts, racquetball courts, etc. In some instances, you just need to show your ID and sign up for the court. If the sport is popular on campus, you might also be given a time limit in order to accommodate all the students wishing to use the facilities. Using the sports facilities is a good way to meet new friends who share a common interest: sports.

Vocabulary

range of emotions [reindʒ əv iˈməuʃən] 情感

frightened [ˈfraitnd] adj. 害怕的，受恐吓的

anxious [ˈæŋkʃəs] adj. 焦虑的

accustomed [əˈkʌstəmd] adj. 习惯

surroundings [səˈraundiŋz] n. 环境

routine [ruːˈtiːn] n. 程序，日常工作

nerve-wracking [ˈnəːvˌriækiŋ] adj. 极端令人头疼的，非常伤脑筋的

nerves [nəːvz] n. 神经 v. 鼓起勇气

beneficial [ˌbeniˈfiʃəl] adj. 有利的，有益的

skip [skip] v. 跳跃，遗漏

mindset [ˈmaindset] n. 观念模式，思维倾向，心态

tolerated [ˈtɔləreitid] adj. 容忍的

responsibilities [riˌspɔnsəˈbilitiz] n. 责任（pˈ 形式）

appointment [əˈpɔintmənt] n. 约会；任命；职务；职位

license [ˈlaisəns] n. 执照，许可证

hurdle [ˈhəːdl] n. 栏，跳栏 v. 克服

community [kəˈmjuːniti] n. 社区，团体

punctual [ˈpʌŋktʃuəl] adj. 准时的

lateness [ˈleitnis] n. 迟，晚

aside [əˈsaid] adv. 在旁边，撇开

newness [ˈnjuːnis] n. 新，新奇

clinic [ˈklinik] n. 诊所，门诊部

routine [ruːˈtiːn] n. 例行公事；日常工作；固定节目 adj. 例行的；常规的；

physical examination [ˈfizikəl igˌzæmiˈneiʃən] n. 身体检查；健康检查

temperature [ˈtempəritʃə] n. 温度；体温；气温

lungs [lʌnz] n. 肺；呼吸器官

reflexes ['ri:ˌfleksiz] n. 反应能力，反射作用（reflex 的名词复数）

tapping ['tæpiŋ] v. 开发（tap 的现在分词）；轻拍，轻敲

kneecaps ['ni:kæps] n. 膝盖骨，护膝（kneecap 的名词复数）

diabetes [ˌdaiə'bi:tis, -ti:z]n. ＜医＞糖尿病

anemia [ə'ni:mi:ə] n. 贫血症

expedite ['ekspiˌdait] vt. 加快进展；迅速完成

purposes ['pə:pəsiz] n. 意志（purpose 的名词复数）；目的；作用；（进行中的）行动

facilities [fə'silitiz] n. 工具；（学习、做事的）天资；设备（facility 的名词复数）

tasks [tɑ:sks] n. 工作，任务，差事（task 的名词复数）

librarian [lai'brɛəriən] n. 图书管理员

overdue [ˌəuvə'dju:] adj. 过期的；延误的，迟到的；未兑的；早应完成的

periodicals [ˌpiəri'ɔdikəlz] n. 期刊（periodical 的名词复数）

journals ['dʒə:nlz] n. 期刊；日志

back stacks [bæk stæks] n. 过期刊物

food plan [fu:d plæn] 饮食计划

microchip ['maikrəˌtʃip] n. 微晶片

purchased ['pə:tʃəst] adj. 购买的，买到的 v. 购买（purchase 的过去式和过去分词）

reads [ri:dz] v. 读，看懂，理解（read 的第三人称单数）；显示，标明

cashier [kæ'ʃiə] n. 出纳员 vt. 解雇；抛弃

debit card ['debit kɑ:d] n. 借记卡，签帐卡，提款卡

social ['səuʃəl] adj. 社会的，社会上的；交际的，社交的 n. 联谊会，联欢会

phenomenon [fi'nɔminən,fə'nɔminən] n. 现象，事件；奇迹；非凡的人

shocked [ʃɔkt] adj. 惊愕的，受震惊的 v. 使…震惊（shock 的过去式和过去分词）

buffet-style ['bʌfit stail] n. 自助式

hence [hens] adv. 因此，所以；从此；从此处

crazy ['kreizi] adj. 疯狂的；不理智的；离奇的；生气的

gained [geind] v. 获得（gain 的过去式和过去分词）；赢得；增加

avoided [ə'vɔidid] v. 避开，避免，预防（avoid 的过去式和过去分词）；

gaining ['geiniŋ] v. 获得（gain 的现在分词）；赢得；增加

workout ['wɜːk,aʊt] n. 锻炼，练习；试验

track [træk] n. 小路，小道；痕迹，踪迹；轨道，音轨；方针，路线

athletic [æθ'letik] adj. 运动员的；运动的；体格健壮的；行动敏捷的

handball ['hændbɔːl] n. 手球

racquetball ['rækitbɔːl] n. 短网拍墙球，手球式墙球

instances ['instənsiz] n. 例子，实例（instance 的名词复数）

accommodate [ə'kɔmədeit] vt. 容纳；使适应；向…提供住处；帮忙

Conversation Questions

If you wanted to, when could you fit in more study time?

What do you fear most about next semester's classes?

What was your biggest fear before you began your next year of college?

How much of the course material is covered by the professors in your classes?

During classes, do you like working in student groups or working alone? Why?

What are some advantages of studying alone? Disadvantages?

What are some advantages of studying in groups? Disadvantages?

Do you prefer to study with friends/classmates or to study alone?

Do you have easy access to your professors outside of class?

How often do you read ahead for your classes?

Discussion Questions

Do you get really nervous when you are doing something new for the first time?

Can you think of any other ways to learn more about the campus?

Would it be easier to rely on your friends or do it all by yourself?

How long will it take you to adjust to campus life?

How long did it take you to adjust to campus life in China?

What was the most difficult part of campus life in China for you?

Do you think campus life in a western country will be the same? Why?

What kinds of activities do you think they will have?

Can you think of other ways to calm yourself down?

Can you imagine what your first day would be like? Explain.

Practice Dialogues

Throughout this book you will have a variety of dialogues that you can use to practice speaking and asking questions. Each section of the book will have 3 dialogues for your use.

Dialogue # 1 – 2 Students

A: Excuse me, can you tell me where the dining hall is?

B: Sure. See that brick building over there, well that is the dining hall.

A: Thanks. I am new and I had no idea where it was located.

B: My name is Wendy. I am a senior this year and it looks like we are in the same dorm.

A: Nice to meet you Wendy. I am _____. I just came here from China.

B: Well it's nice to meet you as well. Listen, I was about to go over to the dining hall after I drop off my books in my room. Would you like to go over and have lunch with me?

A: That would be great, if it isn't too much trouble for you.

B: No trouble at all. I just need to run up to my room and drop these on the bed. I'll be back in a few minutes.

A: Okay, I will wait here for you.

B: See, that didn't take long. Now, let's go to lunch!

A: I haven't been to the dining hall yet. I've been eating in my room since I got here.

B: You mean no one showed you where the dining hall was?

A: No one. I didn't want to bother anyone.

B: Well, that will have to change. When you need something you must speak up or you will not get it.

A: I see.

B: Well, I can show you around the campus if you like. I have no more classes today and plenty of time to study this evening.

A: That would be wonderful. Thank you so much.

B: My pleasure. But first, let's eat lunch.

A: I brought along my student ID just in case.

B: Lucky you. You will need it to pay for lunch.

A: That's what I thought.

B: Ready to go inside?

A: Yes, I am so hungry today.

B: Well, once you see what is in the dining hall, you will soon forget that you are hungry at all.

A: Oh my, look at all the food!

B: This is what it looks like every day.

A: Really? They always put out this much food?

B: Yes. There are many students on this campus.

A: I guess there are. So, how does this work?

B: Just follow me.

A: Okay.

Dialogue #2 – Same 2 students

B: So, did you have enough to eat?

A: My God, I've never eaten so much food in my life.

B: Like I said, it is this way every day, three times a day.

A: I feel guilty.

B: Why?

A: I was thinking about my home and the school I went to before. The food we had to eat was very little and not as good as this.

B: I see. But you can't think about the past. You are in the US, not back

in China. One day the kids in that school you went to will have plenty of food to eat. You can't worry about it now.

A: I guess you are right. But I will not overeat like I did today.

B: Just remember the Freshmen 15 and you will stop yourself from eating too much.

A: Oh, that's the amount of weight new students' gain during their first year at the university, right?

B: Correct. You've been talking to someone.

A: My dorm-mate. She told me about it a few days ago. I thought she was kidding. Now I know it is true!

B: Students come to the school from all kinds of families. Some are rich, others are poor. The students use food to get through their homesickness. It is a way for them to cope with being away from family and friends.

A: That makes sense.

B: You are thousands of miles from your home. You will be homesick from time to time. I would suggest that when you feel homesick, go outside and take a walk. Take a few pictures and send them home to your parents.

A: That's a nice idea. I do miss them, but everything here is so exciting and new that I only think of them when I slow down.

B: That's normal around here. We are always on the go. Speaking of on the go, let's take a tour of the school.

A: Okay, lead on Wendy.

Dialogue #3 – Same 2 students

A: What is that building over there?

B: Which one?

A: The large glass one.

B: Oh, that the gym. The glass section is the pool area.

A: A pool?

B: Yes. Are you a swimmer?

A: Back home I would swim as much as I could. I love swimming.

B: Well, if you enjoy it so much perhaps you should sign up for the swim team.

A: Me, on a swim team? That is too crazy!

B: Why? Most of the students on the team swim because they enjoy it. They practice almost every day and the best ones are selected for the swim meets.

A: I really do enjoy swimming. I think I will tryout for the team.

B: There you go. You'll be winning races in no time. Plus swimming will keep you in shape and the Freshmen 15 will only be a memory.

A: True, very true.

B: The building in the center of the school is the library. There are 6 floors in the building. The first floor is mainly references and a place to sit and relax after class.

A: I thought talking was forbidden in the library?

B: If you are on the other floors, they don't want you to speak too loudly. But the first floor has a special place set up for students coming from classes. It's like a meeting area.

A: Really? That sounds different.

B: Let's go and have a look.

A: Okay.

B: See. This is the Commons area. Students come here to hang out and relax. They can sit and talk, have something to eat or drink or even

sleep if they like. The only thing the school will not allow is loud music since it is in the library.

A: Makes sense. I like the idea of having a place where you can just sit and relax after class.

B: So do a lot of students. We used to go to the dining hall, but they kicked us out because there were too many students just hanging around.

A: So the school set up this place?

B: No, this place has always been here. There are other places on campus where students hang out after classes.

A: Oh, I see.

B: Okay, that small white building over there is the clinic.

A: I know that one. I was there on my second day here.

B: Physical exam, right?

A: Yes. It was okay.

B: The people in the clinic are very nice and always professional. I don't go there very often, but when I have to go, they have always been nice to me.

A: That's good to know.

B: Now we are back at the dorm, and I need to start my studies. I have a big paper due in a few days.

A: Well, thank you Wendy for the tour and for going to lunch with me. Good luck with the paper.

B: And good luck with the swim team. Talk to you soon?

A: Okay, bye.

B: Bye.

Chapter 5
Study Tips for University Success

求学篇场景对话攻略

Guided Reading

如何让你的大学生活很快有立足之地，如何和老师、同学相处，如何更好完成你的学业，在这一章里你可以看到你想要的。

As a new student in a foreign country, you will find yourself at times trying to do things as you would have at home. Studying for classes is one of them. Most Chinese students have been taught to study alone and that by doing so they get the maximum benefits from it. Unfortunately, this is not true. In secondary school, the teacher spoke and students listened. In the university setting, it is quite different. Every teacher has his/her own way of conducting class, and you will find these methods are at odds with the way you were taught at home.

Some classes are set up in circles, with the teacher sitting in the circle with the students. Everyone in the class is equal, even the teacher. This allows students to speak freely about the topic at hand. Other classes are set up in a more traditional way with students listening to a teacher giving a lecture. This type of classroom usually ends with a series of questions being asked by the students. However, in this setting, not every student is heard.

For you to be successful in your university life, you need to change your methods of study. The first thing you need to do is form a study group. Every class you take should have a study group for it. The best number of students in a study group is four. You have three people to talk to and to listen to. You share your ideas about something and they offer criticism or advice. It makes learning the subject much easier and more efficient.

So, form a group. How could you, form a group? The easiest way is to ask people. If you are a shy person, you could advertise it on the campus bulletin boards. Just put the subject, teacher and class time on a piece of paper. Inform everyone you are setting up a study group and that you are looking for three people.

Study groups are necessary because they allow you to voice your opinion and to discuss out loud your thoughts on any subject you are taking.

If you need to write something for class, you have six more eyes to read your words. They can be as critical as you wish and by being critical they will help you become a better writer. You, in turn, become a set of eyes for the others in your group. You read their papers, criticize how they write and eventually your perception of their skills will change your own skills. This is a win-win situation for everyone.

Listed below are several ways to make your time at the university more productive and successful:

Study and Homework Groups　加入学习小组和家庭作业小组

Never underestimate the power of your peers, especially when working through a difficult problem set or reading assignment. Dividing and conquering is an effective way to reduce your workload -- and to make sure you understand the material. You might even make a friend in the process.

Alternate Study Spaces　适当变换学习的地点

Although some people swear by the library, cognitive scientists suggest that alternating study spaces is a more effective way to retain information, according to New York Times. Memory is colored by location, and changing your study location increases the likelihood of remembering what you've learned.

Make Flash Cards　用小卡片辅助记忆

Sometimes the best habits are the ones we've used forever. Flash cards are oldies but goodies — writing notes and definitions more than once will help imprint information in your memory, and the cards are a great way to develop and use mnemonic devices and associative phrases.

Go To Class 正常上课

This one might seem obvious, but large lectures and early start-times often make class feel, shall we say, optional. The best way to prepare for tests is to attend classes and participate.

Don't Immerse Yourself in Subject Material 不要过度专注于一个科目

In keeping with the age-old proverb that values quality over quantity, scientists have found that immersion is not an effective method of study, which is reported by New York Times. Rather than sticking to one subject and spending hours attempting to master it, you should switch between a few (related) topics. It's less boring -- and you'll learn more.

Manage Your Time 合理安排时间

The only thing worse than having a deadline is missing a deadline. Stay organized, cut down on procrastination and your work load will feel much more manageable.

Sleep! 充足的睡眠

A tired mind is a slow mind. Get enough sleep and watch your GPA rise.

买书：

中国，书的价格基本是按照这本书字数的多少而定价的，美国则不是这样。美国的书无关字数多少，它看的是这本书的文化知识价值，文化知识价值越大，那么这本书就越贵，这也导致留美的学生们，对于买教科书，买辅导书很是头疼。

现在的高书价，NYU 一门戏剧课，22 本书，一共 2000 多美元，在这么一个通胀风险随时存在的年头，教育的投资价值也慢慢成为市场上一个不可避免的争论。任何人都不能否认教育的重要性，但是教育究竟重要到什么程度，什么样的投资回报率是合理的，恐怕很难有谁给出个合理的解释。

去美国读书,一门课动辄开出十几本、几十本书的 reading list,在知识产权同样面临通胀的今天,学会买书,也能够间接地增加学位的价值。印书是过去学生用的好办法之一。过去网店不怎么发达,二手书的渠道也相当有限。一本三百页左右、上百美元的书在 Office Depot 的 copy center 印下来,差不多十几块就能搞定。只是出了钱你还要搭上至少半天的功夫,而且万一在复印过程中你把页码顺序搞错了,那就更有的忙了。

那么,怎么样才能摆脱这种让我们中国留学生穷迫的境况呢?下面来说几个方法:

第一:可以问上一个年级的学长学姐们借,交付一定的费用,但是这种情况还是相对比较少的。

第二:美国有些书店出售二手书,这些书有可能是以前的学生卖给书店的。这时候,二手书的价格虽不能说便宜,但相较之前,肯定是便宜了很多。

第三:对于绝大多数学生来说,最方便省钱的途径还是图书馆。美国各个学校的图书馆藏书量都相当了得。常用教学、参考书目基本上都能找得到。而且一本书通常情况下至少能够外借两个月甚至更长,外加续借一次的服务基本上把整个学期都 cover 上了。对于很多常用书籍,即使是本校没有多余馆藏,学生还可以根据各个大学图书馆之间开设的"Interlibrary Loan"跨院借书,从周边其他院校的图书馆馆藏申请借阅。而服务所需的所有运费成本也完全有学校承担。

面对高价的教科书、辅导书、借书、买二手书、到图书馆借书成了很好的节约留美费用的方法。但是图书馆借书也有不方便的地方,再多的 copy,图书馆毕竟不是书店,开学没几天,去的稍微晚一点,你要找的书肯定都被借光了。

此外,图书馆的书通常版本跟不上教授的要求,落后 2-3 个版本一点不稀奇。对于商科和理工科这类要求与时俱进的专业而言,这就意味着,即便你能借到你需要的书,还是很有可能因为版本落后,找不到指定版本对应的页面或是由于内容滞后而不得不到书店去买一本最新版本。

在美国的几大连锁书店中,做的最大的实体店是 Barnes and Noble 和 Border's,BN 从加盟店的数量上感觉规模要更大一点。这两家都属于那种能在美国电影中见到的、喝着咖啡品书的地方。BN 在大多数的校园内也开设了分店，专门销售该大学的教学用书及学校纪念品等。

在实体店买书的优势在于能够看到实物，在购买之前详细地了解书的内容，而且一旦退课或是换课，能够在最短的时间把书退还给书店，方便回收资金。

当然，现在是网络信息的时代，网上购书或者购买电子书也成为了一种流行，网站推出了相关电子阅读器的插件。希望通过软件的兼容性来尽可能地提高电子图书的销售量。但是，考虑到个人阅读习惯以及电子图书的特点，也许并不是每个人都适合购买电子书、特别是电子教科书。从经济成本上考虑，购买或是租借电子教科书也未见得划算。

最经济的办法还是几个人分享一本。这样，几年大学下来根本就没买过几本课本，节约了不少费用。

选课：

留美的同学，进入美国校园的第一件事，就是选课，很有意思也很艰难。由于中美教育体系与教学方法上的不同，再加上语言的隔阂，在留学生活初期，来自课业上的无形压力多少令人感到吃不消。

选课本身可说是一门必修课，课程选择适当与否将是影响学期成绩的最大关键。刚开始就读的第一个学期，特别要注意课不要选得太多、太重，以免为自己带来沉重的课业负担。虽然学校规定修满十二个学分的学生才被承认为全时学生（Full – Time Student）身份，但是若觉得负担太重，可以跟指导教授讨论少修一门课，并请他在有关文件上签名，再向注册组报备，便可继续保持全时学生身份。

有关课程内容的资料，在开学之前就应着手收集。例如参阅学校各系目录（Catalog）上的课程简介（Course Description）或是参考课程时间表（Course Schedule）等等，都可以得知自己系上所开的课程。

在选课时最重要的两点，就是一定要了解课程内容和主讲教授。最好事先了解课程内容是否对你有用、你是否感兴趣、教授教研水平如何、为人如何、教学方式如何等等。

1、课程进度表

由于普通的课程简介通常相当简略,若想知道更详细的课程内容,一定要主动到系办公室直接询问开课的教授或其助教、秘书。同时,索取该课程整个学期的上课计划进度表(Syllabus),上面列有详尽的课程目标、每次上课进度、评分标准,以及书单等等项目,可说是选课时最实际的参考。

2、教授的名声

学生对教授的评论是选课时另一重要考量因素。有时某门课的名称、内容相当吸引人,但若打听出该教授是个"Killer",可考虑放弃该门课。所谓"杀手"教授通常会布置很多考试、作业,而且分数给的不高,一般而言并不受学生欢迎。当然,有心在学术上有所建树的同学,可以着重考察教授的学术能力和观念等等。

开学之后,正式上课或旁听更可印证自己选课选得如何。如果上课时发现该课程并不符合自己需要、太难或者旁听时对其他课程产生兴趣,都应该当机立断尽快办理改选手续。通常在开学前某一特定时间内加、退选都不收取费用。

Note Taking – 如何做笔记

One of the best ways to become successful in school is by taking good notes.

Taking notes is a great way of helping you identify important concepts in class. Even if you have a great memory, you won't be able to remember everything that the teacher says.

Here is an example about a literature lecture: The purpose of a literature lecture is often to offer important background information about the literature you're studying, including: biography, literary history, period and movement details, discussion of relevant literary terms, details about the author's style, thematic relationships between works, critical perspective on the works, important quotations, or other relevant material related to the work, time period, etc. The content from literature lectures usually has a way of appearing in mysterious ways in quizzes, in-class writing assignments, essay assignments, and other testing situations. Even if the lecture material doesn't reappear in a testing situation, you may be asked to draw from the knowledge you gained from the lecture for a future in-class discussion, and it's just a good idea to have a record of what you've covered so far in the class. So, here are a few tips about what to think about as you take notes in your literature class.

Before Class 课前准备

To prepare for your next class, read the assigned reading material, which is often listed on the course outline. It's usually a good idea to read the material a day before the reading assignment is due. If possible, you'll want to read the selection several times, and make sure you understand what you're reading. If you have any questions, your textbook may offer a list of suggested readings to help with your understanding. A visit to your library may also offer additional reference resources to answer your questions, and further prepare you for class. Your notes from previous class periods may also help to answer your questions.

Also, be sure to take a look at the "Questions for Consideration," whether they are from your professor or in your textbook. The questions often help you to re-evaluate the text, and they may help you to understand how the material relates to other works you've read in the course.

课前准备与课后复习：
在正式上课之前，课前的预习是很重要的准备工作。上课前多花点时间认真

阅读必要的教科书和参考书，预先对教授所要讲的内容作到心里有底，这对于我们英语非母语的中国学生来说尤其重要。只有这样，你才能比较多地理解教授在课堂上的讲述，也能够比较容易地加入同学们的讨论。

课前及课后充分的阅读准备，将有助于课堂内容的有效吸收。一般而言，研究生课程进度相当快，尤其暑期（Summer Session）的课程时常压得人喘不过气来。面对在短期内要读完的好几本教科书及指定读物，如何训练自己的阅读速度便成了十分重要的课题。

阅读英文书时最好不要逐字诵读，这样不但速度缓慢，也不容易找出文章里的关键所在。阅读时应该随时提笔，记下自己所学专业领域的字汇及术语，而且每读一个段落，应做摘要笔记，或是标示出重要关键词。

此外，最好能训练自己用简单英文表述大意——一来方便日后复习，二来更能练习使用英文表达，以增加课堂上发言的信心。每当阅读英文书籍时，常会遇到一大堆单词，而令人产生"词到用时方恨少"的感慨。更有甚者，即使查出所有单字的意义，却仍对整句词语一知半解，让人相当气馁。

为了增进自己的阅读速度及能力，最好不要太拘泥于字句的推敲钻研，而应以掌握全段、全文大纲为努力的方向。预习、复习时，有时候可以使用中文相关书籍来辅助英文书籍的阅读，以掌握概念。但是中文书籍的辅助毕竟只是权宜之计，唯有在平时就能充实自己的英文阅读能力，才能吸收更多专业领域的新知。

During the Literature Class 课堂上应该如何记笔记

Be prepared to take notes when you attend your class; and be on time. That means... bring plenty of paper and pens with you.

Write down the relevant date, time, and topic details on your note paper before the teacher is ready to start. If homework is due, hand it in before the class starts, and then be ready to take notes.

Listen carefully to what the teacher says. Particularly note any discussion about future homework assignments and/or tests. The teacher may also give you an outline of what he or she will discuss for that day. Remember that you don't have to get down every word that your teacher says. Get enough notes so that you can understand what was said. If there's something that you don't understand, be sure to mark those sections so you can come back to them later.

As you take notes, pay special attention to signal words: "First, Second, Next, Then, Thus, Another important..." Your teacher will often let you know where he or she is at in the lecture, and more importantly, what material you should take special note of.

Since you've read the reading material before class, you should recognize new material: details about the text, the author, the time period, or the genre that wasn't covered in your textbook. You'll want to get as much of this material down as possible, because it's material that the teacher probably considers important to your understanding of the texts.

Even if the lecture seems disorganized, or hard to understand, get down as many notes as possible through the lecture. Where there are gaps, or parts of the lecture you don't understand, you want to clarify your understanding of the material by: asking questions in class or in the teacher's office hour, asking a classmate for clarification on a point, or finding outside reading materials that may further explicate the issue. Sometimes, when you hear the material in a different way, you may understand the concept much more clearly than when the first time you heard it. Also, remember, every student learns in a different way. Sometimes, it's better to get a more broad perspective--from various sources, both in and out of class.

Don't be in a rush. You're probably scheduled to sit in the class for at least an hour, and the teacher will probably take full advantage of the time.

Listen carefully. Take careful note of what the teacher says. Don't let yourself zone out. You may be missing out on information that you're going to need for a future test or literature paper.

If you know you have a hard time paying attention, try some preventative measures. Some students find that chewing on gum or a pen helps them to pay attention. Of course, if you're not allowed to chew gum in the class, then that option is out... but find a way to pay attention. It's important!

- Esther Lombardi, About.c om Guide

课堂行为：

不论托福听力成绩有多高，几乎每位留学生刚开始上课时都经历过一段"鸭子听雷"的茫然。如此一来便影响课堂上的反应，以及抄笔记的速度。除了尽快设法熟悉每位教授不同的口音及讲话方式外，录音或笔记都可以帮助自己，但需注意下列几点：

1、录音

上课时即使听得再认真、笔记做得再勤快，也不免有疏失之处。这时候，录音机就成为温习功课、补充笔记的最大帮手。但录音之前一定要征求教授的同意，因为牵涉到版权或其他问题，有些教授并不欢迎学生录音。此外，必须避免对录音过分依赖，不要以为录音后回家可以反复再听，而影响上课专心的态度。

2、笔记

除了自己预习、复习时的笔记之外，上课所记的笔记常常是课程的精华、考试时参考的宝典。大致说来，一至二个学期下来，留学生就能培养出记笔记"简单扼要、层次分明"的功力。如果教授喜欢写黑板，对记笔记的帮助当然很大；若是讲演或讨论的课，则需特别留意"There are some important points..."、"This is the key which..."或是"I'd like you to remember..."等类似的开场白,它们几乎都是上课重点所在。

此外,还要学习能够过滤出课堂重点,假若教授或同学发言时说些无关紧要的话,当然就不必有闻必记了。如果笔记一直无法抄得好,应该设法跟其他同学借来参考,甚至直接向教授反映。通常教授会指派助教或特定同学协助。有了上课完整的笔记,预习、复习功课时更能如虎添翼。

3、学习用品

在国内的很多上课习惯在这里可能会被完全打破。随之而来的是在使用学习文具用品上也有了很大的不同。在这里,向大家推荐一些文具,在笔者看来是必备的,并且给将来的学习、复习和考试会带来相当的益处。大号文件夹(A4 Level Arch File,WHSmith,0.99镑或1.99镑),塑料文件套(通常100个2到3镑),小型文件打孔机(puncher)和订书机(stamper),彩色粘性便笺纸簿(中-13cm x 8cm 小-5cm x 8cm),铅笔和至少三种颜色的圆珠笔或彩笔,外加粗号的加重笔(highlight),等等。老师经常会在课上发一些notes,而你自己也经常会上网找到一些有帮助的信息后打印出来,所以及时的整理每门课的学习资料就非常重要,有了上述的文具,相信不会很难吧!

4、发言

上课时的发言,不但能与教授及其他同学做多向交流,也能充分表现出学生的参与感,进而在教授心中留下好印象。中国学生通常在课堂上表现较为沉默,许多留学生担心自己英语不够好、害怕出洋相而不敢发言。事实上,人都已经越洋留学了,又何必过分担心出洋相呢?如果觉得自己英语能力不强,上课发言不正是训练自己用英语表达的好机会吗?虽说如此,如何突破心理障碍而踊跃参与课堂讨论,却仍是留学生最需要努力克服的问题。

美国学生从小即习惯于表达自己的意见,随时能侃侃而谈。但他们也习惯接纳别人发表意见,一旦外国学生发言,他们通常会耐心听完。

刚开始若真不知如何表达，不妨先就上课听不懂、听不清楚的地方提出疑问，例如可以举手向教授表示："I can't follow you."或是"Can you say that again？"。当然，最好是能逐渐去除恐惧的心理，进而勇敢积极地在课堂上发表自己的看法，才能达到思想交流的目的。

5、课后提问

在这个国家，老师确实是个很自由的职业，另外，相当的老师可能还有做研究的重任，因此在课后找老师解答上课有疑问的地方也不是那么地 简单。但是如果你掌握一定的方法（如电子邮件预约、和有关秘书预约、打电话给老师等），在通常情况下，经常的课后提问会让老师留下一个好印象，尤其如果你还能有自己独到的见解，说不定老师还会让你参加什么科研项目呢！当然，最主要的还是通过课后的提问，把上课没有记录下来的重点或是没有听清的部分和老师澄清。这样，在做课后的作业时就方便多了。

考试、习题与报告：

在经过一学期紧张的学习之后，接下来的就是学习测评了。评价学习成果的主要方式，不外乎大小考试、作业习题与书面、口头报告等，并不是每位教授都选择同样的方式。

1、考试

期中、期末两次大考，成绩比重约占全学期60%以上，因此每到考试期间，大家都挑灯夜战，不敢掉以轻心。若是在课堂上考试，最好问清楚各种细节，如考试形式、内容、范围等。考试若采取申论题的形式，如果担心时间不够使用，可尝试向教授要求延长作答时间。此外，更应问明是否能携带英汉或汉英字典进场作答。另外，一种拿回家完成的考试（Take Home Exam），由于没有时间等方面的严格限制，一般来讲压力不大。只要根据上课笔记、指定书籍内容发挥，再注意词句的连贯与修饰，获得满意的成绩应该不难。

2、指定作业（Assignment）

不同的科系有不同方式的作业习题。大致说来，数理商等系的作业以计算、应用题方式较为常见，只要上课用心听讲，再参考教科书及笔记，或跟同学、学长讨论，这种作业多半难不倒你。而人文社会科系的作业，通常是指定阅读和书面报告，这种作业较偏重评论、分析和表达。

除此之外，口头报告（Presentation）可能是压力最大的一种作业形式。由于上课时要在教授及其他同学面前用英文报告，所以文稿的拟定必须特别清楚流畅；而面对随时可能被教授或同学打岔和质疑，常会令人神经紧张。然而，准备这种作业的方式，唯有融会贯通，并且熟记自己所拟的文稿内容，并事先请其他同学"试听"一下，才能让自己正式提出报告时从容不迫。

3、学期报告（Term Paper）

有许多教授喜欢以学期报告取代考试来评价学生的学习成果,因此,有关撰写学期报告的各种细节也不容忽视。为了避免自己写的报告格式不符合教授要求，最好事先能向教授索取一分报告样本，依照其各种规定来写，才万无一失。例如多数心理系同学必须遵守APA（美国心理协会）所发行的报告格式书写，丝毫不得马虎。在美国留学，写学期报告时千万不能小看著作权的问题，凡是引用别人的资料或言词，必须详细注明，以免被冠上"剽窃"的罪名，轻则受低分处分，严重时更遭退学的命运。如果能随时注意引用原句时要加上引号，以及注明原文作者、书名及页数，即可避免抄袭之嫌。（这和我们中国大大不同）

着手进行学期报告时，有任何疑问或想法意见都可在教授办公时间（Office Hour）与其商讨。如在报告截止日期前写完，不妨先拿去跟教授讨论，一方面有利于报告整体的修改，另外也可增加教授的印象。在Office Hour会见教授，是学生的基本权利，万不可以怕麻烦教授为由，而放弃了自己的权益。

撰写学期报告时，首重内容品质，而不是文字的华美。所以只要文法正确、主旨突出、文意连贯并且清楚明了，就算是一篇上乘的报告。

然而，对自己的英文能力无论抱持多大的信心，最好还是请美国同学或花钱聘请人帮忙修改英文文法、修辞，甚至全文组织，以使整篇报告更加圆润通顺。

留学生活虽不尽如"游学"般轻松惬意，但是只要熟悉了与课业相关的"游戏规则"，读书得法，留学生也能时时忙里偷闲的。

Vocabulary

maximum ['mæksiməm] adj. 最高的；最多的；最大极限的

conducting [kən'dʌkt] v. 指挥；指导

taught [tɔːt] v. 教授（teach 的过去分词）

equal ['ikwəl] n. 同辈；相等的事物

freely ['friːli] adv. 自由地；直率地

criticism ['kritə'sizəm] n. 批评

efficient [i'fiʃənt] adj. 有效率的

voice [vɔis] vt. 表达

perception [pə'sepʃn] n. 看法；洞察力

underestimate [ʌndər'estimeit] vt. 低估；看轻

peer [pir] n. 平辈，同龄人

conquering ['kɔŋkə] v. 战胜，征服；攻克

reduce [ri'djuːs] vt. 减少；降低

workload ['wɜːkləʊd] n. 工作量

material [mə'tiəriəl] n. 材料

cognitive ['kɔgnətiv] adj. 认知的，认识的

alternating ['ɔltɚˌnet] v. 使交替；依次变换（alternate 的 ing 形式）

retain [ri'tein] vt. 保持；记住

New York Times 纽约时报

locale [ləʊˈkɑːl] n. 场所，现场

likelihood [ˈlaiklihʊd] n. 可能性，可能

imprint [imˈprint] vt. 刻上记号

mnemonic [niˈmɔnik] adj. 记忆的；助记的；记忆术的

device [diˈvais] n. 装置；策略

associative [əˈsəʊʃiətiv] adj. 联想的

phrases [freiz] n. 短语，习语

optional [ˈɔpʃənəl] adj. 可选择的，随意的

proverb [ˈprɔvɜːb] n. 谚语，格言；众所周知的人或事

quality [ˈkwɔliti] n. 质量

quantity [ˈkwɔntiti] n. 量，数量

immersion [iˈmɜːʃən] n. 沉浸；专心

switch [switʃ] v. 转换

deadline [ˈdedlain] n. 截止期限，最后期限

procrastination [prəu,kræstəˈneʃən] n. 耽搁，拖延

manageable [ˈmænidʒəbl] adj. 易管理的；易控制的

GPA 平均成绩积点 (Grade Point Average)

identify [aiˈdentifai] v. 确定；识别

concept [ˈkɔnsept] n. 观念，概念

background [ˈbækɡraʊnd] adj. 背景的

biography [baiˈɔɡrəfi] n. 传记；个人简介

literary history 文学史

relevant [ˈrelivənt] adj. 有关的；中肯的；有重大作用的

thematic [θiˈmætik] adj. 主题的，主旋律的

critical [ˈkritikəl] adj. 评论的

perspective [pəˈspektiv] n. 观点

quotation [kwəʊˈteiʃən] n. 引用语；引证

mysterious [mi'stiəriəs] adj. 神秘的；不可思议的
situation [sitjʊ'eiʃən] n. 情况；形势
reappear [riːə'piə] v. 再出现
assigned [ə'saind] adj. 指定的；已分配的
suggested [sə'dʒɛstid] adj. 建议的；暗示的
resource [ri'sɔːs] n. 资源
previous ['priːviəs] adj. 以前的
reevaluate [,riːi'væljueit] v. 再评估；重新估计
relate [ri'leit] v. 与……有某种联系
recognize ['rɛkəg'naiz] v. 认出，识别
genre ['ʒɔŋrə] n. 类型；流派
disorganized [dis'ɔrɡənaizd] adj. 紊乱的；无组织的
gap [gæp] n. 间隙；缺口；空白
clarify ['klærifai] v. 澄清；阐明
clarification [,klærəfə'keʃən] n. 澄清，说明
explicate ['eksplikeit] v. 说明，解释
zone out 上课开小差
preventive [pri'ventiv] adj. 预防的，防止的

Conversation Questions

1. How often do you read ahead for your classes?

2. What can/do you do if you fall behind in your classes?

3. Where is the best place for you to study? Why?

4. How much note taking do you do in most of your classes?

5. How often do you reread or organize your notes from a professor's lecture?

6. What are some advantages in studying with sophomore/junior/senior students/friends or with older students?

7. Do you prefer to study with friends/classmates or to study alone?

8. What's your favorite way to take a 'short' break from studying at night?

Practice Dialogues

Throughout this book you will have a variety of dialogues that you can use to practice speaking and asking questions. Each section of the book will have 3 dialogues for your use.

Dialogue # 1 – 2 Students –

A: I am going to the library to study, want to come along?

B: What subjects are you studying?

A: Math and English tonight.

B: Do you study alone or in a group?

A: In a group.

B: Why? Isn't it easier to study by your self?

A: Not really. Being in a group helps me understand what the other students are thinking. I listen to what the teacher says, but sometimes I don't get it. So when I am in my study group we talk about it and try to help each other understand it better.

B: Oh, I see. That makes a lot of sense.

A: This is how it works for me. I take notes in class and when I hear something that isn't clear to me, I put a star beside it and I take it to the

group later.

B: Good system. It works every time?

A: Every time. If we are not sure, as a group, one of us will go to the professor and ask again. Eventually we get the answer we need.

B: Okay, I could use some help with English.

A: What about Math?

B: No, I love math. It is very easy for me.

A: Good. You can help those of us who are struggling to get through the class.

B: Sounds good. I don't mind helping.

A: Great! Let's go.

B: Okay.

Dialogue #2 – Teacher and student –

A: Two weeks from today you will have your first exam. We will cover the first four units of your textbook and the handouts I have given to you up to this point.

B: Excuse me Professor.

A: Yes? Do you have a question?

B: Yes I do. Will the test also cover the assigned readings?

A: It might.

B: So what you are saying is that we should look over the assigned readings just in case they appear on the exam?

A: That would be a good idea.

B: Thank you.

A: You are welcome. Now, any more questions?

B: One more professor.

A: Okay, go ahead.

B: Can you tell us how much this exam counts toward our final grade?

A: If you had taken the time to read your syllabus, you would see that this exam counts for 25% of your overall grade.

B: Okay, thank you.

A: Right. Any other questions? No? So, turn to page 52…

Appendix A
Dialogues

求学篇场景对话攻略

场景 1: Preparing to Depart

Dialogue #1 – Student and Embassy/Consulate Official

Officer: Hello, how are you today?

Student: I am fine. Thank you.

Officer: Good. Shall we get started?

Student: Okay, I am ready when you are.

Officer: Please tell me your full name.

Student: My name is _____.

Officer: Can you tell me where you were born?

Student: Yes, I was born in _____, in China.

Officer: And how old are you?

Student: I am _____ years old.

Officer: When will you be traveling abroad?

Student: I plan to leave during the summer, in July or August, before classes begin at the university.

Officer: What school will you be going to?

Student: I will be attending the University of _____.

Officer: And what will you study at the university?

Student: I will study _____.

Officer: How long will you be in the U.S.?

Student: I will be in the U.S. for 4 years unless I decide to get my Masters too. Then I will be there for 6 years.

Officer: Very good. Thank you for your answers. I hope you have a safe trip and enjoy your time in the U.S..

Student: Thank you very much.

Dialogue # 2 – Two students talking

Student 1: So, are you ready for your big trip to the U.S.?

Student 2: Almost, but I feel like I am forgetting something.

Student 1: Did you make a list of all the things you need to take along?

Student 2: Yes, I have completed the list.

Student 1: Well, if you have any problems or you find that you left something behind, send me an email and I will send it to you.

Student 2: Oh that would be great. I don't know if I have forgotten something or if I am just nervous about the trip.

Student 1: I think you are just nervous about the trip.

Student 2: Yes, but I am also excited about it too.

Student 1: Wells you should be. This is once-in-a-lifetime opportunity.

Student 2: I know it is. And I am determining to make the most of it.

Student 1: You will do well and make lots of new friends when you get there.

Student 2: I have already made some new friends at the university. I was given their email addresses and I have been talking to them for 3 weeks now.

Student 1: That's great. So when you get there they will be waiting for you?

Student 2: Oh yes. They said they would pick me up at the airport after I go through Customs.

Student 1: Have you filled out all the paperwork for the university?

Student 2: Yes and no. I have sent almost everything to them, but I am waiting for my final grades here to send along to them. I told them the grades would be sent as soon as possible.

Student 1: Were they okay with that?

Student 2: Yes, they completely understand.

Student 1: Well, I will miss you so much. You must promise to write to me every week.

Student 2: I will. Plus we can chat from time to time on QQ or Skype.

Student 1: Okay. Now let's get you to the airport before you miss your flight.

Dialogue #3 – Student and Teacher

Teacher: Are you ready to go?

Student: I guess so. I have everything packed.

Teacher: When do you leave?

Student: I leave tomorrow morning at 9:15.

Teacher: How long will the flight be?

Student: They said it would take 12 hours.

Teacher: So you will arrive in the evening and you will be tired.

Student: Yes, after the plane lands they said it takes about 45 minutes to get through Customs and pick up the baggage.

Teacher: Will there be someone waiting for you?

Student: Yes, a few of the students from my dorm will meet me.

Teacher: That's good. Are you excited about the trip?

Student: Oh yes. I am very excited about it but it is hard to sleep at night.

Teacher: Well, make sure you sleep on the flight over. If you do not, you will be very tired.

Student: I have never been on a plane before, so I don't know if I will be able to sleep. Perhaps when it gets dark I will be able to sleep.

Teacher: Well, I hope you have a wonderful time at your new school. Please write to me and tell me what is happening in your life over there.

Student: I will write to you as often as I can.

Teacher: Good luck in your studies. If you have any difficulties, let me know and I will try to help you.

Student: Thank you for your kindness. I will keep that in mind.

Teacher: Good bye, have a safe trip.

Student: Thank you. I will see you next summer when I come home.

Teacher: Okay. We can sit and talk about your new life in America.

场景 2: Arriving and Settling In

Dialogue # 1 – Student and Customs Agent

Customs Agent: Next please. Please step up to the line.

Student: Okay. What do you want me to do?

Customs Agent: Please hand me your passport and the form you filled out on the airplane.

Student: Okay. Here are my papers.

Customs Agent: So, what country are you from?

Student: I am from China.

Customs Agent: And what brings you to the United States?

Student: I am here to study at the university.

Customs Agent: Did you bring any items with you that might be harmful? Such as food items or plants?

Student: No. Just my clothes and my computer for school.

Customs Agent: Okay, now I need you to go to the next area and you will be searched.

Student: Okay. Thank you for your help.

Customs Agent 2: Full body scan or strip search, which one would you prefer?

Student: I do not know.

Customs Agent 2: The full body scan is faster if you are in a hurry.

Student: Okay, let's do that one.

Customs Agent 2: Right. Walk through the area ahead and the machine will scan your body.

Student: Okay, thank you.

Customs Agent 2: Not at all.

Dialogue #2 – Meeting at the Airport

Susan: Hi, my name is Susan. I am from the university and I've come to pick you up.

Student: Hello. My name is _____. Very nice to meet you Susan.

Susan: I see you have your bags. Is there anything else we need to get for you before we leave the airport?

Student: No, I went through Customs, the scanning and got all my luggage. I am ready to go.

Susan: Great! Let's get out of here.

Student: Where are we heading now?

Susan: Well, first we will go back to the university. Once we get there, you will have some time to unpack and relax. I have a short meeting to attend and then we will take a tour of the campus.

Student: Sounds good to me.

Susan: Are you hungry?

Student: Not really. I ate on the plane. We had enough food because it was a long flight.

Susan: How long was your flight?

Student: I left Shanghai yesterday, so it took about 14 hours altogether.

Susan: Wow, you must really be tired now.

Student: I am tired, but I am also excited about being in America.

Susan: Most new students feel the same way. I hope you like here.

Student: Me too. I think it will be fun and exciting.

Susan: Well, it will take us about 1 hour to get to the university, so sit back and relax. It's a nice sunny day so you can see a lot of the city as we drive through it.

Student: I think I will take some pictures on the way to send back home to my parents.

Susan: Good idea. You can show them that you have arrived safe and sound.

Student: Yes.

Dialogue #3 – Student and Resident Advisor

RA: Hi, you must be _____ from China?

Student: Yes, I am.

RA: Well, my name is Jessica. I am the Resident Advisor for this building. You can call me Jessica. I am also a student here. I am working on my Masters in Child Psychology.

Student: Hello Jessica. My name is _____. I will be studying _____ here at the university.

RA: Well, let me show you to your room and tell you a bit about the dormitory and what goes on around here.

Student: Okay. Thank you.

RA: Here is your room. You have one roommate. You've already met her. Her name is Susan. She picked you up at the airport. Susan is in a meeting right now but will be back to take you on a tour in about 2 hours.

Student: Good. So we have 2 beds, desks, computers and our own bathroom?

RA: Yes. This is typical housing at the university. We also have a few students living alone.

Student: Wow. In China we have 6 to 8 students sharing a room half this size.

RA: That is crazy. There are some universities that put 4 students in a room, but the rooms are not small. It's like a bedroom with a living room and study room. So there is plenty of space for 4 students.

Student: Can you tell me where I can do my laundry?

RA: Sure. Downstairs in the basement we have several washing machines and dryers. When you need to use one ask Susan. She can show you where they are located.

Student: Great. Thank you so much.

RA: A few rules for you. No loud music, no smoking or drinking in the dorm. We all like to have a quiet place to live, so if you want to listen to music just put on some headphones.

Student: Sounds good to me. Thanks Jessica.

场景 3: Orientation and Scheduling/Choosing classes

Dialogue # 1 – 2 Students

A: Hi, what's your name?

B: My name is _____.

A: So, where are you from?

B: I'm from China.

A: How long have you been in the US?

B: Just for a few days now.

A: Any thoughts about our country? The people? The school?

B: I haven't had much time to sit and think about everything. Orientation is moving quickly.

A: I know what you mean. My name is Sasha. I'm from Russia.

B: Nice to meet you Sasha. How long have you been here?

A: Oh, I arrived last week.

B: Do you like it here?

A: Oh yes. The school is really large and the other students have been very kind and helpful to me.

B: Well that's good to know. I hope we can become good friends this year.

A: I think we will. Say, what classes are you taking this semester?

B: I'm not sure yet. I think I have to take the basic classes like everyone else.

A: Well, we should register for the same classes and then we can study together.

B: That sounds like a good idea. They told me that I should find other people to study with since we do not study in groups back in China.

A: The only way to get through the courses is to study in a group. You can use other's opinions to help you figure things out.

B: Sounds good to me. Let's go register when the orientation is over.

A: Okay.

Dialogue #2 – Student with Registration Official

Student: Excuse me. I need to register for classes.

R.O.: Okay. Do you have your student ID with you?

Student: Yes, here it is.

R.O.: Good. Now, since you are a new student and this is your first year, you need to take at least 15 credits of classes. You can take up to 18 if you wish. Any number of credits higher than 18 would have to be approved by the head of the department for your major. Do you understand?

Student: I think so. If not, I will ask as we go along.

R.O.: That's a good idea.

Student: So all I have to do is to follow the guidelines for my major and take the basic classes that the department has outlined in the student handbook?

R.O.: Yes and no. You need to take the basic classes for the first 2 years. Afterwards, you concentrate on your major for the final 2 years. When you choose the basic courses you want, you also must take some electives. The electives can be anything that is of interest to you. However, you might want to choose courses that would help you in your major. Like computers.

Student: Oh, I see. Yes, a computer class would be useful since I will be doing a lot of writing this year. Thanks for the information.

R.O.: Not at all. Just come back if you have any problems or questions.

Student: Okay, thanks again. Bye.

R.O.: Bye.

Dialogue #3 – Student in the Bookstore

Clerk: Okay, who is next?

Student: That would be me.

Clerk: Let me see your class schedule and student ID, please.

Student: Here you go.

Clerk: So, you are a freshman and you are majoring in Business.

Student: That's right.

Clerk: See that sign hanging from the ceiling over there? That is the Business area. All your textbooks for Business will be there. But first, you need to get your basic classes out of the way.

Student: Tell me where I should go first.

Clerk: Start at the top of your schedule and work your way down. Looks like English is the first one and those books are over there on your left. Just look at the signs hanging from the ceiling. Go to each section you need and if you can't find what you need, ask the person working in that section. They will help you out.

Student: Okay. English first on the left, then on to the other sections. So, Business is last on my list?

Clerk: It is your major and you will have only introductory classes in Business for the first 2 years. You only need a few books from that section now. Eventually all your books will be from that section.

Student: Got it. Thanks for your help.

Clerk: No problem. Good luck with your classes.

Student: Thanks.

场景 4：Getting around the Campus

Dialogue # 1 – 2 Students

A: Excuse me, can you tell me where the dining hall is?

B: Sure. See that brick building over there, well that is the dining hall.

A: Thanks. I am new and I had no idea where it was located.

B: My name is Wendy. I am a senior this year and it looks like we are in the same dorm.

A: Nice to meet you Wendy. I am _____. I just came here from China.

B: Well it's nice to meet you as well. Listen, I was about to go over to the dining hall after I drop off my books in my room. Would you like to go over and have lunch with me?

A: That would be great, if it isn't too much trouble for you.

B: No trouble at all. I just need to run up to my room and drop these on the bed. I'll be back in a few minutes.

A: Okay, I will wait here for you.

B: See, that didn't take long. Now, let's go to lunch!

A: I haven't been to the dining hall yet. I've been eating in my room since I got here.

B: You mean no one showed you where the dining hall was?

A: No one. I didn't want to bother anyone.

B: Well, that will have to change. When you need something you must speak up or you will not get it.

A: I see.

B: Well, I can show you around the campus if you like. I have no more classes today and plenty of time to study this evening.

A: That would be wonderful. Thank you so much.

B: My pleasure. But first, let's eat lunch.

A: I brought along my student ID just in case.

B: Lucky you. You will need it to pay for lunch.

A: That's what I thought.

B: Ready to go inside?

A: Yes, I am so hungry today.

B: Well, once you see what is in the dining hall, you will soon forget that you are hungry at all.

A: Oh my, look at all the food!

B: This is what it looks like every day.

A: Really? They always put out this much food?

B: Yes. There are many students on this campus.

A: I guess there are. So, how does this work?

B: Just follow me.

A: Okay.

Dialogue #2 – Same 2 students

B: So, did you have enough to eat?

A: My God, I've never eaten so much food in my life.

B: Like I said, it is this way every day, three times a day.

A: I feel guilty.

B: Why?

A: I was thinking about my home and the school I went to before. The food we had to eat was very little and not as good as this.

B: I see. But you can't think about the past. You are in the US, not back in China. One day the kids in that school you went to will have plenty of food to eat. You can't worry about it now.

A: I guess you are right. But I will not overeat like I did today.

B: Just remember the 'Freshmen 15' and you will stop yourself from eating too much.

A: Oh, that's the amount of weight new students' gain during their first year at the university, right?

B: Correct. You've been talking to someone.

A: My dorm-mate. She told me about it a few days ago. I thought she was kidding. Now I know it is true!

B: Students come to the school from all kinds of families. Some are rich, others are poor. The students use food to get through their homesickness. It is a way for them to cope with being away from family and friends.

A: That makes sense.

B: You are thousands of miles from your home. You will be homesick from time to time. I would suggest that when you feel homesick, go outside and take a walk. Take a few pictures and send them home to your parents.

A: That's a nice idea. I do miss them, but everything here is so exciting and new that I only think of them when I slow down.

B: That's normal around here. We are always on the go. Speaking of on the go, let's take a tour of the school.

A: Okay, lead on Wendy.

Dialogue #3 – Same 2 students

A: What is that building over there?

B: Which one?

A: The large glass one.

B: Oh, that the gym. The glass section is the pool area.

A: A pool?

B: Yes. Are you a swimmer?

A: Back home I would swim as much as I could. I love swimming.

B: Well, if you enjoy it so much perhaps you should sign up for the swim team.

A: Me, on a swim team? That is too crazy!

B: Why? Most of the students on the team swim because they enjoy it. They practice almost every day and the best ones are selected for the swim meets.

A: I really do enjoy swimming. I think I will tryout for the team.

B: There you go. You'll be winning races in no time. Plus swimming will keep you in shape and the Freshmen 15 will only be a memory.

A: True, very true.

B: The building in the center of the school is the library. There are 6 floors in the building. The first floor is mainly references and a place to sit and relax after class.

A: I thought talking was forbidden in the library?

B: If you are on the other floors, they don't want you to speak too loudly. But the first floor has a special place set up for students coming from classes. It's like a meeting area.

A: Really? That sounds different.

B: Let's go and have a look.

A: Okay.

B: See. This is the Commons area. Students come here to hang out and relax. They can sit and talk, have something to eat or drink or even sleep if they like. The only thing the school will not allow is loud music since it is in the library.

A: Makes sense. I like the idea of having a place where you can just sit and relax after class.

B: So do a lot of students. We used to go to the dining hall, but they kicked us out because there were too many students just hanging around.

A: So the school set up this place?

B: No, this place has always been here. There are other places on campus where students hang out after classes.

A: Oh, I see.

B: Okay, that small white building over there is the clinic.

A: I know that one. I was there on my second day here.

B: Physical exam, right?

A: Yes. It was okay.

B: The people in the clinic are very nice and always professional. I don't go there very often, but when I have to go, they have always been nice to me.

A: That's good to know.

B: Now we are back at the dorm, and I need to start my studies. I have a big paper due in a few days.

A: Well, thank you Wendy for the tour and for going to lunch with me. Good luck with the paper.

B: And good luck with the swim team. Talk to you soon?

A: Okay, bye.

B: Bye.

场景 5： Study Tips for University Success

Dialogue # 1 – 2 Students –

A: I am going to the library to study, want to come along?

B: What subjects are you studying?

A: Math and English tonight.

B: Do you study alone or in a group?

A: In a group.

B: Why? Isn't it easier to study by your self?

A: Not really. Being in a group helps me understand what the other students are thinking. I listen to what the teacher says, but sometimes I don't get it. So when I am in my study group we talk about it and try to help each other understand it better.

B: Oh, I see. That makes a lot of sense.

A: This is how it works for me. I take notes in class and when I hear something that isn't clear to me, I put a star beside it and I take it to the group later.

B: Good system. It works every time?

A: Every time. If we are not sure, as a group, one of us will go to the professor and ask again. Eventually we get the answer we need.

B: Okay, I could use some help with English.

A: What about Math?

B: No, I love math. It is very easy for me.

A: Good. You can help those of us who are struggling to get through the class.

B: Sounds good. I don't mind helping.

A: Great! Let's go.

B: Okay.

Dialogue #2 – Teacher and student –

A: Two weeks from today you will have your first exam. We will cover the first four units of your textbook and the handouts I have given to you up to this point.

B: Excuse me Professor.

A: Yes? Do you have a question?

B: Yes I do. Will the test also cover the assigned readings?

A: It might.

B: So what you are saying is that we should look over the assigned readings just in case they appear on the exam?

A: That would be a good idea.

B: Thank you.

A: You are welcome. Now, any more questions?

B: One more professor.

A: Okay, go ahead.

B: Can you tell us how much this exam counts toward our final grade?

A: If you had taken the time to read your syllabus, you would see that this exam counts for 25% of your overall grade.

B: Okay, thank you.

A: Right. Any other questions? No? So, turn to page 52.......

Appendix B
Tables & Forms

各类申请表格

表一入学申请表

ADMISSION SECTION
PRINT CLEARLY IN BLACK INK

Name of Institution	City/Province	Country	Dates Attended From To	Graduation Date

Social Security Number _____ Your Social Security Number will be a student identifier. Please enter it here if you have one.

Full Legal Name _____

Permanent Address _____

City _____ Country/State _____ ZIP _____

County/Province _____ Date of Birth _____

Phone Cell _____

Receive text messages from University? Yes o No o Email _____

Program Type

New freshman

No o

Transfer with less than 24 semester hours

Transfer student

Postgraduate (degree seeking)

High school concurrent

Transient (visiting student)

National Student Exchange

Non degree seeking

Mr. o   Mrs. o   Ms. o   Dr. o

Ethnicity and Race*

Are you Hispanic/Latino? Yes o

Choose appropriate race. Check all that apply.

American Indian/Alaskan Native

Asian

Native Hawaiian or Other Pacific Islander

Black or African-American

White

Not disclosed

Parent/Guardian/Spouse Contact _____

Relationship _____ Phone _____

Address _____

City_____ Country/State _____ ZIP _____
Email _____
Cell phone _____ Receive text messages from University? Yes o   No o
Student's Full Name

_____   _____
        Last or family name   Given name
MI _____ Social Security Number (if available)
List High School or Prep School
List all high schools attended. Grades or marks are needed for years 9–12 and beyond.
Name_____
Address _____

Dates attended _____   _____
From   To
Graduation _____
date
List courses to be completed during your senior year of high school (freshmen only). (The University course requirements are a factor in the admissions process.)
Have you previously enrolled at this university? Yes o No o
Student number_____
LIST ALL COLLEGES ATTENDED OR THAT YOU PLAN TO ATTEND BEFORE ENROLLING AT THIS UNIVERSITY.
Attach an additional sheet if necessary. An official transcript from each college must be submitted to the Admissions Office at the university.
Note: If there is a break of more than one term in your education, please attach a statement of activity.
If you answer yes to any of the following questions, please attach a separate sheet of paper stating the approximate date and explaining the circumstances of each incident.
DISCIPLINARY/CRIMINAL HISTORY
1. Have you ever been found responsible for a disciplinary violation, academic or behavioral, at a college, university or other postsecondary institution which resulted in your probation, suspension, removal, dismissal or expulsion? Yes o No o

2. Have you ever been convicted of, pled guilty to or pled no contest to a felony or sexual offense? Yes o No o

3. Are you currently the subject of pending charges or an indictment, or subject to arrest, for any criminal offense, including felonies or lesser offenses? Yes o No o

4. At the time of your entry to UA, will you have been separated from the U.S. Armed Forces, National Guard or Reserves with a dishonorable or bad conduct discharge or been dismissed by sentence of a general court-martial or sentenced to confinement adjudged by a court-martial or in a federal or state penitentiary or correctional institution? Yes o No o

I certify that I have complied with the provisions of the United States Military Selective Service Act (50 U.S.C. App 453) by registering with the Selective Service Board or that I am not yet 18 years of age and I will register when required or that I am not required by law to register. (This certification is required by State of Alabama Legislative Act 91-584.) I certify that all information given in this application is complete and accurate. I understand that withholding information requested or giving false information may make me ineligible for admission and enrollment or subject to suspension.

Capstone Creed: As a member of the University of Alabama community, I will pursue knowledge; act with fairness, honesty, and respect;

foster individual and civic responsibility; and strive for excellence.

Applicant's signature (full legal name) _____

美国海关出入境登记表（I-94 FORM）（中英文对照）	
U.S. Department of Justice OMR 1115-4077 Immigration and Naturalization service	美国司法部 OMR 1115-407 移民局
Welcome to the United State	欢迎来到美国
Admission Number **697385031 01**	登记号码（*举例说明） **697385031 01**
I-94 Arrival/Departure Record-Instructions	I-94 入境 / 离境记录说明
This form must be completed by all persons except U.S. citizens, returning resident aliens with immigrant visas, and Canadian Citizens visiting or in transit.	除了美国公民，美国海外侨民，和访问或过路的加拿大公民外，所有人士都必须填写此表。
Type or print legibly with pen in ALL CAPITAL LETTERS. Use English. Do not write on the back of this form.	请用大写字母打字或用钢笔或用圆珠笔清楚填写，请用英文填写，不要在此表背面填写任何东西。
This form is in two parts. Please complete both the Arrival Record (Item 1 through 13) and the Departure Record (Item 14 through 17).	此表包括两部分，请填写入境记录（第 1 项至第 13 项）和离境记录（第 14 项至第 17 项）两部分。
When all items are completed, present this form to the U.S. Immigration and Naturalization Service Inspector.	填写完毕后，请将此表交给美国移民局官员。
Item 7 – If you are entering the United States by land, enter LAND in this space. If you are entering the United States by ship, enter SEA in this space.	第 7 项内容说明□□□□□如果你从陆地进入美国，请在空格内填写 LAND，如果你乘船进入美国，请在空格内填写 SEA。
Form I-94(10-01-85)N	I-94 表 (10-01-85)N
Admission Number **697385031 01** Immigration and Naturalization Service	登记号码 **697385031 01** 移民局

I-94	I-94
Arrival Record	入境记录
1. Family Name	1. 姓
2. First (Given) Name	2. 名
3. Birth Date(Day/Mo/Yr)	3. 生日（月／日／年）
4. Country of Citizenship	4. 哪个国家公民
5. Sex (Male or Female)	5. 性别（男填 MALE 或女填 FEMALE）
6. Passport Number	6. 护照号码
7. Airline & Flight Number	7. 航空公司和航班号
8. Country Where You Live	8. 你在哪个国家生活
9. City Where You Boarded	9. 你在那个城市降落
10. City Where Visa Was Issued	10. 在哪个城市得到签证
11. Date Issued (Day/Mo/Yr)	11. 得到签证的日期（日／月／年）
12. Address While in the United State (Number and Street)	12. 在美国的住址（门牌号及街名）
13. City and State	13. 在美国的住址（市名及州名）
Departure Number	离境号码
697385031 01	**697385031 01**
Immigration and Naturalization Service	移民局
I-94	I-94
Departure Record	离境记录
14. Family Name	14. 姓
15. First (Given) Name	15. 名
16. Birth Date(Day/Mo/Yr)	16. 生日（日／月／年）
17. County of Citizenship	17. 哪个国家公民

美国海关申报 /Custom Declaration Form （中英文对照）	
WELCOME TO THE UNITED STATES	欢迎来到美国
DEPARTMENT OF THE TREASURY UNITED STATES CUSTOMS SERVICE	财政部 美国海关署
CUSTOM DECLARATION	海关申报
1. Name: Last First Middle Initial	1．姓名： 姓 名 中间名（首字线）
2. Number of family members traveling with you	2．与你同行的家庭成员人数：
3. Date of Birth: Month Day Year	3．出生日期： 月 日 年
4. Airline/Flight:	4．航空公司／航班号：
5. U.S. Address:	5．在美居住地址：

6. I am a U.S. Citizen YES NO If No, Country:	6. 你是一个美国公民吗 是 否 如果不是，你是那个国家的公民：
7. I reside permanently in the U.S. YES NO If No, Expected Length of Stay:	7. 你是在美国永久居留吗 是 否 如果不是，预期停留多久：
8. The purpose of my trip is or was **BUSINESS PLEASURE**	8. 此次旅程的目的是 商务旅游
9. I am/we are bringing fruits, plants,meats, food, soil, birds, snails, otherlive animals, farm products, or I/we have been on a farm or ranch outsidethe U.S. Y E S NO	9. 你携带水果，植物，肉类，食品，土壤，鸟类，蜗牛，其他动物和农产品，或你一直居住在美国以外的农村或牧场吗 是 否
10. I am/we are carrying currency or monetary instruments over $10000U.S. or the foreign equiralent. Y E S NO	10. 你携带现金或珍贵物品，其价值超过一万美金或相当于一万美金的外币吗 是 否
11. The total value of all goods I/we purchased or acquired abroad and am/are bringing to the U.S. is (see instructions under Merchandise on reverse side; visitors should report value of gifts only):$_____ U.S. Dollars	11. 你境外购买或获得并带入美国所有物品总价值（参看背面商品栏目；访问者只须申报礼品价值）:$ ___ 美元
SIGN ON RESERSE SIDE AFTER YOU READ WARNING.(Do not write below this line.)	在你阅读警告之后请在背面签字（不要在此线下面签字）
INSPECTOR'S NAME STAMP AREA	检察员姓名 盖章区域
BADGE NO.	徽章号码

Appendix B
Word Bank

词汇表

acceptance	bargain	credits
accommodate	behave	critical
accompany	biography	criticism
according	bloom	curriculum
accustomed	boarding pass	customs
acquainted	Bon voyage	deadline
add/drop	bookstore	deadlines
additional	bored	debit card
advisor	buffet-style	decision
aisle	bulletin board	destination
alternating	cashier	devices
ample	challenge	difficult
anemia	clarification	disliked
appendix	clarify	disorganized
appointment	clearly	diverse
aside	clinic	document
assigned	cognitive	effect
assistance	community	efficient
associative	complaint	electronic
athletic	concepts	electronic age
attached	condition	emergency
attachment	conducting	encounter
attempt	confusing	enhance
avoided	conquering	equal
back stacks	consult	essay
background	contact	ethnic
baggage claim	crazy	ethnicity

exception	handbook	mention
excitement	hence	merely
expedite	hungry	microchip
explicate	hurdle	mindset
facilities	identifies	minnesota
familiar	identify	mixture
Federal Law	immersion	mnemonic
file	imprint	morning person
financial	instances	mysterious
financial aid	institution	nerves
flexible	issues	nerve-wracking
food plan	jot	nervousness
freely	journal	new-found
frightened	journey	newness
full body scan	kneecap	newspaper
gained	knowledge	optional
gaining	lateness	orientation
gaps	librarian	original
generated	likelihood	overdue
genre	literary history	panic
gladly	locales	paperwork
GPA	lung	passport
graduate	manageable	pat-down
grant	material	peer
guide	maximum	percentage
gymnasium	medically	perception
handball	memory	periodicals

permanent	quantity	seatbelt
perspective	quotations	security check
pertinent	race	self-confidence
phenomenon	racquetball	self-confident
phrase	range of emotions	shock
physical examination	reappear	signal
pinyin	recognize	situation
possible	record	skip
practice	reduce	social
prefer	reevaluate	specialty
preventive	refer	specific
previous	referee	stamped
primarily	reflex	status
process	registered	Student Number
processing fee	relate	student visa
procrastination	representative	submit
profound	request	submitted
program	requirement	sufficient
proof	resident	suggested
prove	resource	surrounding
proverb	responsibility	switch
provides	retain	tapping
publication	roam	tardiness
purchase	roster	tardy
purchased	routine	task
purpose	scan	taught
quality	scholarship	temperature

temporary

terminal

terminology

time-consuming

tolerated

track

transcript

transfer

transient

translated

tuition

underestimate

uniform

unpacking

upcoming

variety

venture

version

via

visa

voice

weapon

wisdom

workload

workout

work-study

zone out

普通高等教育"十二五"规划教材

留美学习与生活情景对话 下册

生活篇

Fly Away

（美）Michael Kussmaul 杜曾慧◎主编

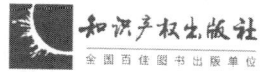
知识产权出版社
全国百佳图书出版单位

内容提要

本书分为上下两册,重点注重于语言的运用能力,为读者构建了一个个实际的语言情景,每章都是以场景的形式出现,有知识类的介绍,词汇总结、相应的话题讨论,和典型情景对话范例,既适合阅读者自己阅读学习,也适合用于英语教学。本书上册为学习篇,主要致力于出国前的各项准备及新生入学后的注意事项。例如,如何申请国外大学,国际航班注意事项、新生入校后如何参加学校的各项活动及其注意事项等;下册为生活篇,主要致力于学校的课外活动,生活上可能遇见的问题及如何处理这些问题。如美国钱币知识的介绍,学生证及护照、在学校餐厅和校外就餐等生活常识。

责任编辑: 于晓菲 许波　　**责任出版:** 陆运霞 刘译文

图书在版编目(CIP)数据

留美学习与生活情景对话(上、下)-Fly Away/(美)Michael Kussmaul,杜曾慧主编.—北京:知识产权出版社,2013.04
　　ISBN 978-7-5130-1932-3
　　Ⅰ.①F… Ⅱ.①杜… Ⅲ.①留学教育-英语 Ⅳ.①H31
　　中国版本图书馆CIP数据核字(2013)第046647号

留美学习与生活情景对话(下)(生活篇)——Fly Away
LIUMEI XUEXI YU SHENGHUO QINGJING DUIHUA (XIA) (SHENGHUOPIAN)

(美) Michael Kussmaul　杜曾慧　主编

出版发行: 知识产权出版社	
社　址: 北京市海淀区马甸南村1号	邮　编: 100088
网　址: http://www.ipph.cn	邮　箱: rqyuxiaofei@163.com
发行电话: 010-82000893 转8101	传　真: 010-82005070/82000893
责编电话: 010-82000860 转8363	责编邮箱: yuxiaofei@cnipr.com
印　刷: 北京中献拓方科技发展有限公司	经　销: 新华书店及相关销售网点
开　本: 720mm×960mm 1/16	印　张: 20.25(上、下册)
版　次: 2013年4月第1版	印　次: 2013年4月第1次
字　数: 308千字(上、下册)	定　价: 42.00元(上、下册)

ISBN 978-7-5130-1932-3/H·099 (4775)

出版权专有　侵权必究
如有印装质量问题,本社负责调换。

《留美学习与生活情景对话（生活篇）——Fly Away》编委会

主　编：（美）Michael Kussmaul　杜曾慧

副主编：李玉霞　张劲柏　余音　任李

Table of Contents

Chapter 1　Student Activities
　　　　　　学生活动 /1

Chapter 2　Getting Around the City or Town
　　　　　　熟悉新地方 /29

Chapter 3　Dining Out
　　　　　　外出就餐 /51

Chapter 4　Contacts and facing problems /solving problems
　　　　　　紧急联系电话及面对问题 / 解决问题 /77

Chapter 5　American Holidays
　　　　　　美国的节假日 /95

Chapter 6　American Money&Student ID and Passport
　　　　　　美元和学生证 / 护照问题 /125

Appendix A – Dialogues　生活场景对话攻略 /137

Appendix B – Word Bank　词汇表 /159

Chapter 1
Student Activities
学生活动

Guided Reading

大学里的各种活动五彩斑斓，其目的是拓展知识、提高能力、完善素质、陶冶情操。每个大学都有自己的一些社团组织，这些组织为大学生搭建了沟通的平台和锻炼自己各种能力的舞台，学生活动形式多样、内容丰富、格调高雅、寓教于乐。

Every university or college in the US has a Student Organization and Student Activity department. The purpose of this department is to allow students to develop as individuals through school-sponsored clubs and activities. Many clubs are registered through this department and no matter what your major field of study might be, there is a club or organization on campus where students share your interests.

Getting involved in these activities will allow you to develop many skills that you will need when you have finished your education and have moved on into the real world. Here are some skills you will be able to develop:

Event Management 事务管理

Student leaders engaged in student activities have a unique opportunity to learn and practice effective event management. Student leaders should strive towards understanding the appropriate steps and issues involved in event planning and management. Some of the most transferable skills - contract negotiation, program planning and event promotion - are developed and honed in this area.

With regards to Event Management, students will:

Understand and practice the steps of effective program programming, implementation, execution and evaluation.

Implement appropriate risk management strategies.

Delegate tasks and hold committee members accountable.

Utilize personnel and financial resources appropriately.

Follow and navigate appropriate institutional policies.

Leadership Development

Leadership involves a broad spectrum of skills and character qualities. Student leaders involved in student activities must understand that their role is to be a positive change agent, to influence others and create a vision. Leadership is a process rather than a position. Leadership is relationship oriented and situational in nature.

With regards to Leadership Development, students will:

Demonstrate growth in problem-solving abilities.

Move their organization toward the mission and strategic goals of the organization.

Understand the skill set of the membership and utilize it effectively for engaging organizational members in accomplishing the group's goals.

Hold self and members accountable.

Recognize the ethical components of leadership.

Interpersonal Relationships 人际关系

Establishing meaningful interpersonal relationships is critical for successful leadership in student activities. Student leaders often rely on committee volunteers to carry out the essential tasks related to providing programs and services. The work of student activities is often supported by several on and off-campus constituencies. Profess ionalism, diplomacy and recognizing the support of others will enhance organizational effectiveness.

With regards to Interpersonal Relationships, students will:

Demonstrate an ability to work with the various departments within the University, especially other units within the Division of Student Affairs.

Establish mutually trustworthy and rewarding relationships with students, faculty and staff, friends, and colleagues.

Listen to and reflect upon others' points of view.

Treat others with respect.

Communication 沟通能力

Effective communication is a critical skill that helps student leaders ensure that their organizations achieve their goals. When communication is a focal point of student learning, individuals will personally benefit and organizations will be run more efficiently.

With regards to Communication, students will:

Demonstrate strong oral and written communication skills.

Convey messages and influence others through writing, speaking, or non-verbal expression.

Develop and facilitate thoughtful presentations.

Work effectively in teams and in multicultural settings.

Express disagreement in respectful and civil ways.

Manage and resolve conflicts that exist among organization members.

Collaboration 互相合作

Collaboration involves seeking the involvement of others and working well with people. Student leaders should actively contribute to the achievement of a group goal. They would seek feedback from others and exhibit growth in their skills as a result of working collaboratively.

With regards to Collaboration, students will:

Demonstrate a basic understanding of meeting management, member recruitment, retention and motivation.

Demonstrate proficiency for utilizing community and professional resources.

Work cooperatively with others, seeking their involvement and feedback.

Utilize delegation as a means to involve group members.

Create formal and informal networks with other student leaders to build awareness of the issues facing their organizations.

Promote and conduct joint programs between organizations.

Intellectual Growth 智力增长

Intellectual Growth is central to the mission of higher education and must be a focus in all endeavors inside and outside the classroom. Student activities offers a fertile practice field for intellectual development when student leaders and programmers engage in critical thinking, problem solving and decision making. Student leaders should be cognizant of this learning opportunity and apply knowledge learned to enhance organizational goals and personal development.

With regards to Intellectual Growth, students will:

Apply previously understood information and concepts to a new situation or setting.

Produce personal and educational goal statements.

Use complex information from a variety of sources including personal experience and observation to form a decision or opinion.

Make connections between campus involvement and curricular studies.

Demonstrate an ability to apply skills obtained as members of organizations and how they are used in real world applications.

In addition to honing your own skills, you will gain many new friendships and experiences. So, what kinds of clubs and activities are available to you on campus? That depends on the school you attend, but every school has many clubs and activities to choose from. Here is a list of some of the clubs that may be offered at your school:

参加各类学生活动益处多多，大家想好参加什么社团组织了吗？下面我们不妨来了解一下国外大学的一些社团组织其各自的特点吧！

Club Name	Description
African Student Union	The primary goal of the African Student Union is to spread awareness about the different African cultures. They strive to overcome stereotypes and create unity within our community. The club also dedicates its time to support a variety of African charities.

American Marketing Assoc.

The purpose of this club is to enhance interested students' knowledge about the marketing industry and careers.

Asian Student Association (ASA)

The Asian Student Association seeks to promote the appreciation and understanding of Asia through social, educational and cultural activities. ASA is a unified student body that does not consist of members solely of Asian descent.

Association for Computing Machinery (ACM)

The chapter is organized and operated exclusively for educational and scientific purposes to promote the increasing of knowledge of and greater interest in the science, design, development, construction, languages, management, and applications of modern computing, and as a means of communication between persons having an interest in computing.

Basketball (Men's) Men's Club	Basketball is a group designed to deliver a competitive basketball atmosphere within the confines of the average college student.
Basketball (Women's)	The club is for people who want a fun and competitive environment. They also fundraise and volunteer in the community.
Biology Club	Biology Club is meant to connect those who are biology majors or interested in biology to resources in the department and school to further their interest. It helps connect people who are majors to scientific opportunities inside and outside the university.
Class Council	Class Council coordinates and maintains all traditional class-wide events. Our non-profit organization functions as a separate entity from Student Government Association. The intention of Class Council is to provide inexpensive social activities for the student body.

Cheerleading

The goal of the Cheerleading Club is to promote school spirit by cheering for men's and women's varsity basketball. All skill levels are welcome to join.

Circle K International

Circle K is the college level of Key Club. They are a tight-knit, enthusiastic community service club focused on three tenants of leadership, fellowship and service.

Ecology Club

The Ecology Club is for students with an interest in Ecology and the environment.

Economics Club

The Economics Club is a club open to all students which holds enjoyable economics-related events.

Future Business Leaders of America (FBLA)

FBLA is an opportunity for students to get more involved with the business major. They help clubs market on campus, host leadership activities, and volunteer.

Geography Club

Spreading the love and knowledge of all things Geography!

German Club

The German Club's purpose is to promote the German language and culture in a fun and educational way.

Mathematical Association of America

The MAA student group works closely with faculty, mathematics majors, and any mathematically-inclined students in hosting activities advancing interest in all aspects of mathematics. The student group of the MAA is affiliated with the national office of the Mathematical Association of America, a professional organization which includes university faculty and students of all levels.

National Society of Collegiate Scholars

NSCS is a student honor society dedicated to leadership and community service. NSCS holds many charity events and hosts spirit weeks. It is an active on-campus presence to members and non-members alike.

Outdoors Club	Outdoors Club is geared towards group outings that are organized by the club officers. Trips include kayaking, canoeing, rock climbing, hiking, camping and rafting.
Performing Arts Club	The Performing Arts Club offers performance, choreography, and leadership opportunities in dance.
Soccer (Men's)	Playing soccer in a less competitive environment, while having fun. Soccer is part of the Intramural Program.
Soccer (Women's)	Playing soccer in a less competitive environment, while having fun. Soccer is part of the Intramural Program.
Society of Pre-Law	The Society of Pre-Law is a student organization for those interested in the field of law. The purpose is to network, prepare, and surround ourselves with other students interested in pursuing legal work.

Society of Physics Students

The Society of Physics Students aims to teach, remind, and explore physics through on and off campus lectures, experiments, and workshops. There are activities for majors and non-majors alike.

Sociology and Anthropology Society

The Sociology and Anthropology Society provides a social forum for students interested in these disciplines to meet and explore related issues.

Student Art Association

To promote and support student art on campus and in the surrounding community

Student Government Association (SGA)

The SGA is a forum where students bring their concerns about campus issues ranging from academics to safety. SGA is the students' link with the administration.

Swim Club

Swim Club is for new and old swimmers to exercise and compete together, as well as bond outside of the pool. If your school has a pool.

Tennis Club

The Tennis Club strives to maintain and enhance tennis skills in a fun, competitive, team-building environment at college. They play many schools in the area throughout the year.

UNICEF

UNICEF USA is an international organization dedicated to the "believe in zero." 21,000 children die each day from preventable deaths, and the UNICEF mission is to make that number zero. The purpose of this club is to fundraise for the children, educate the community, and advocate for children of other countries.

Vegetarian Society   A club for vegetarians, vegans, and anyone interested in helping animals. The goals include maintaining a strong vegetarian presence on campus, raising money for animal rights groups, and encouraging discussion about animal rights issues.

Every university in the US knows the importance of establishing clubs and activities for students. They all offer a wide variety of choices. The list above is just a sample of clubs being offered at some universities.

If you are a serious athlete and you want to compete on a more challenging level, every university offers men's and women's athletic activities on the collegiate level nationally. However, if you enjoy a game of ping pong or tennis with friends, you might want to consider joining the Intramural Program at your school. Intramurals are sporting events that are for fun and not taken too seriously. The main objective is to build team leadership and still have a good time. Sports such as softball, football, soccer, tennis, swimming, basketball, etc. can either be set up as a men's team, a women's team or as a co-ed team. If you are not very good at sports but you want to try, this would be a great way to make new friends, have some fun and learn more about the sport.

For students who are more intellectual, there are a few clubs that will be of interest to them. For example, the Literary Club looks at various authors throughout the year. They meet to discuss the writer's work. Most universities have a Chess Club for those of you who enjoy playing chess. If

speaking is your passion, you could join the Public Speaking Club and learn to speak more effectively. When you get settled in at your school, especially in the fall semester, signs will begin to appear alerting every one of club activities. The clubs will be advertising for new members and offering new events.

丰富多采的学生课外活动是美国等许多国家大学的传统，它被视为大学教育有价值的组成部分。但因为大多数学生专业课程任务繁重，只能参加两三项有组织的课外活动。同时课外活动的选择范围很广，通常有剧社、乐队、合唱队、辩论社、电影协会等等。下面是美国大学最流行的九大学生社团，看看哪个是最适合你的？

1. 国际文化俱乐部

许多文化社团的学生都愿意聚集在一起分享自己关于文化的见解同时学习新的文化。日本学生和对日本文化感兴趣的学生会选择参与学校的日本文化俱乐部他们一起讨论日本文化的诸多方面，从日本传统茶道道日本动画。而韩国学生会参与到韩国学生联合会中，并与中国文化俱乐部和越南学生联合会一起参与新年演出活动。这些俱乐部的学生们联合起来就变为了亚洲／亚裔学生联合会，学生们会一起工作并且组织不同的活动。你可以参与一个小组来分享你自己的文化，也可以进入另外一个俱乐部学习一种新的文化。这是一个可以让你遇见不同背景的学生的机会，并从中学习新的文化。

2. 艺术社团

如果你有动听的声音，那么你可以参加合唱团，为整个学校演唱小夜曲。如果你的音乐才华表现在你的指尖，那么也有很多俱乐部适合你。有些学校有韩国打击乐俱乐部、牙买加铜鼓俱乐部，而有些学校甚至还会有口哨合唱团。当然，如果你觉得你属于舞台，也有许多戏剧俱乐部可以供你施展拳脚。这些俱乐部也很适合对灯光、声音控制有兴趣的学生。如果你的朋友经常因为你说的笑话而捧腹大笑时，你可以考虑去参加喜剧社。你可以选择系列小喜剧，这类喜剧要求你事先写出一个故事；你也可以选择即兴喜剧，这会更加考验你的临场应变能力。如果你更加喜欢晃动你的身体，那么舞蹈社团更加适合你。学校中总会有各种各样的舞蹈社团，包括街舞、莎莎、交谊舞等等。这些表演组有不同的级别，试听时对所有人开放。

3. 学术社团

有些学生社团更加倾向于去深入探讨他们在课堂中的学习内容，并且为将来的研究生学习做准备。这些学生通常会成立一个数学、物理或生物俱乐部，通过这样的社团去找寻与自己有相似兴趣的学生并且更加深入了解自己的专业。另外有些学生会通过参与到将来会去法／医／商学院的学生组织的社团中去，来为自己的将来做准备。有些年轻的企业家们可能会成立一个组织在学校中利用一切商机小试牛刀。如果你对政治感兴趣，那么你可以参与模拟联合国。这些社团对你大学毕业以后的生活极其有利。通过这些，你可以结识到很多与你有同样职业规划的人，而且他们总能给你一些关于未来的建议。如果你是对法学院感兴趣的，你可以参与到法律预科学生组织的社团中去，他们可能会在你准备法学院申请的时候祝你一臂之力。

4. 兄弟会／姐妹会

兄弟会姐妹会是校园生活中一个重要的组成部分。兄弟会只有男生，而姐妹会只有女生。当然，有时候也会有两种性别都接受的联谊会。想要参加其中的任何一个，你得先发誓。在大学的第一年里，你需要通过一系列学姐学长们出的测试，让他们判断你是不是适合这个社团。如果你通过了，就可以成为正式的会员。兄弟会经常因为滥用酒精和有一些过于奇特的测试方式（可能会让你做一些尴尬的事情来考验你的决心）而臭名昭著，但是实际情况是，每个社团每个联谊会都有自己的规章制度，而且并不那么的疯狂。参与兄弟会和姐妹会的好处就是它可以帮助你建立一个非常紧密的人际关系网络。你的兄弟或姐妹们会竭力帮助你。你也自动的与校友成员建立了联系。慈善当然也是联谊会生活的重要方面。联谊会总会通过不同的方式为自己的学校或社区服务。大一些的兄弟会可能在不同学校都会有地方分会，这样就可以给你一个更大的人际网络。虽然有时候入会前的测试恐怖了些，但是联谊会生活仍然是帮你建立人际关系网络最好的办法之一。目前美国全国性的男大学生联谊会有150个左右，女大学生联谊会也有65个左右。至于地方性的联谊会则数不胜数。

5. 运动俱乐部 / 校内运动比赛

一些在高中就已经非常出色的运动员在进入大学后决定专心学习而不再在校队中担任职务。而另外一些人只是想和其他同学一起玩玩，并且做些运动。不管你的初衷是什么，总是会有许多运动俱乐部和运动团队适合你。运动俱乐部不需要你像在校队上那样的训练强度，而且任何级别的人都可以参与。如果你想参与到一些激烈的比赛中去，那么学校里各个不同的队伍可能是最好的选择，你可以通过参与其中的一个队伍与你的同学们一比高下。大多数学校有许多美国运动的队伍（篮球、室内足球的队伍），但是很多其他你喜欢的运动可能不是那么普及，例如网球和乒乓球。当然，你也可以召集一群同学成立一个你感兴趣的俱乐部。

6. 活动社团

有一些学生社团是针对某些特定问题而成立的社团。如果你有一个特别关注的问题的话，你可以去寻找一些与你有相同爱好的同学成立一个组织。比如说国际特赦组织会旨在处理美国和国际社会的人权问题。有些学生会去学校的电话中心接一些匿名的电话来帮助那些遇到困难的学生。有些学校会成立专门的组织，来解决性骚扰等问题。"朝鲜自由"组织希望去帮助生活在朝鲜的人们。如果你觉得哪里有不公正的话，那么你就可以去找寻一群与你有相同目标的人。

7. 宗教社团

如果你有兴趣去了解你的精神世界，那么一定会有许多学生组织帮到你。根据不同地域的学生分布，学校里会有很多基督教、天主教、犹太教、穆斯林以及佛教组织。当然也有讨论宗教融合的社团，这些社团希望把不同宗教信仰的人团结起来。就像其他的文化社团，这些俱乐部由不同背景的学生组成，而这些学生想要分享自己的背景并且去接触新的文化。这样的社团可以为提供学生各类意见，从伦理道德问题到如何放松自己。

8. 志愿者

美国实行政教分离的原则，公立院校的课堂设施不能用来宣教，但对学生的课外宗教活动则无限制。一些学校处于人道主义支持位低收入家庭建造房子。另外的会为周边社区提供服务，比如说为周边的初高中学生提供辅导。不同的组织也经常被联合在一起去处理一些突发状况，比如说地震和飓风。你会遇到很多有强烈人道主义观念的学生，也会见到很多伟大的人，同时为社会做一些有用的事情。

9. 其他社团

以上是关于大学社团的一些大致分类。如果你想要的社团没有的话，你可以试着去创建一个，大多数学校支持学生开展新的社团。如果你需要资金的话，你也可以要求学校资助。

在大学里参加的社团就如同你选的课程一样重要，参与学生社团可以为你提供一些你在课堂上遇不到的机会，锻炼自己的能力。找一些你真正感兴趣的社团并且想想你到底从里面学到什么，好好利用这样的机会吧！

Vocabulary

unique [juːˈniːk] adj. 独特的，独一无二的

transferable [trænsˈfɜːrəbl] adj. 可转让的；[数] 可转移的

contract [ˈkɔntrækt] n. 合同

negotiation [nɪgəʊʃiˈeɪʃ(ə)n] n. 谈判；转让；顺利的通过

honed [həʊnd] v. 把…磨光（hone 的过去式及过去分词）

implementation [ˌɪmplɪmenˈteɪʃən] n. [计] 实现；履行；安装启用

execution [ˌeksɪˈkjuːʃ(ə)n] n. 执行，实行；完成；死刑

evaluation [iˌvæljʊˈeʃən] n. 评价；[审计] 评估；估价；求值

risk management   n. 风险管理

delegate [ˈdelɪɡət] vt. 委派…为代表

accountable [əˈkaʊntəb(ə)l] adj. 有责任的；有解释义务的；可解释的

utilize [ˈjuːtəlaɪz] vt. 利用

navigate [ˈnævɪɡeɪt] vt. 驾驶，操纵；使通过；航行于

institutional [ɪnstɪˈtjuːʃ(ə)n(ə)l] adj. 制度的；制度上的；学会的

spectrum [ˈspektrəm] n. 光谱；频谱；范围；余象

character ['kærəktə] n. 性格，品质；特性；角色
situational [sitjʊ'eiʃənəl] adj. 环境形成的；情形的
demonstrate ['demənstreit] vt. 证明；展示；论证
mission ['miʃ(ə)n] n. 使命，任务；代表团；布道
skill set   n. 技能组合
ethical ['eθik(ə)l] adj. 伦理的；道德的；凭处方出售的
components [kəm'pəunənts] n. 部件；组件；成份
leadership ['liːdəʃip] n. 领导能力；领导阶层
interpersonal [intə'pɜːs(ə)n(ə)l] adj. 人际的；人与人之间的
critical ['kritik(ə)l] adj. 鉴定的；爱挑剔的；危险的；决定性的；评论的
essential [i'senʃ(ə)l] adj. 基本的；必要的；本质的；精华的
constituencies [kən'stitjʊənsis] n. 选区；赞助者（constituency 的复数）
professionalism [prə'feʃ(ə)n(ə)liz(ə)m] n. 专业主义；专家的地位；特性或方法
diplomacy [di'pləuməsi] n. 外交；外交手腕；交际手段
effectiveness [ə'fektivnis] n. 效力
within [wið'in] prep. 在…之内
mutually ['mjutʃuəli] adv. 互相地；互助
trustworthy ['trʌs(t)wɜːði] adj. 可靠的；可信赖的
colleagues ['kɔliːgs] n. 同事，同僚
focal ['fəuk(ə)l] adj. 焦点的，在焦点上的
convey [kən'vei] vt. 传达；运输；让与
non-verbal [nɔn'vɜːbəl] adj. 非语言的；非用言语的
facilitate [fə'siliteit] vt. 促进；帮助；使容易
multicultural [mʌlti'kʌltʃ(ə)r(ə)l] adj. 多种文化的；融合或具有多种文化的
civil ['siv(ə)l; –il] adj. 公民的；民间的；文职的；有礼貌的；根据民法的
conflicts ['kɔnflikts] n. 冲突，矛盾；斗争；争执

collaboration [kə,læbə'reʃən] n. 合作；勾结；通敌
seeking [si:k iŋ] v. 寻找；谋求
exhibit [ig'zibit; eg-] vt. 展览；显示；提出（证据等）
collaboratively [kə'læbərətivli] adv. 合作地；协作地
recruitment [ri'kru:tmənt] n. 补充；征募新兵
retention [ri'tenʃ(ə)n] n. 保留；扣留，滞留；记忆力
motivation [,motə'veʃən] n. 动机；积极性；推动
proficiency [prə'fiʃ(ə)nsi] n. 精通，熟练
delegation [deli'geiʃ(ə)n] n. 代表团；授权；委托
means [mi:nz] n. 手段；方法；财产（mean 的复数）
formal ['fɔ:m(ə)l] adj. 正式的；拘谨的；有条理的
informal [in'fɔ:m(ə)l] adj. 非正式的；不拘礼节的
joint [dʒɔint] n. 关节；接缝；接合处，接合点
intellectual [,intə'lektʃuəl; -tjuəl] adj. 智力的；聪明的；理智的
endeavors [in'devəs] n. 努力；尽力
fertile ['fɜ:tail] adj. 富饶的，肥沃的
programmers ['progræmɚs] n. [计][自] 程序设计员
cognizant ['kɔ(g)niz(ə)nt] adj. 审理的；已认知的
enhance [in'hɑ:ns; -hæns; en-] vt. 提高；加强；增加
concepts ['kɔnsepts] n. 观念，概念
complex ['kɔmpleks] adj. 复杂的；合成的
curricular [kə'rikjulə] adj. 课程的
spread [spred] v. 传播，散布；展开；伸展；铺开
awareness [ə'wɛənis] n. 意识，认识；明白，知道
stereotypes ['steriə(υ)taip; 'stiəriə(υ)-] n. 陈腔滥调，老套；铅版
dedicates ['dedikeit] vt. 致力；献身；题献
marketing ['mɑ:kitiŋ] n. 行销，销售

unified ['ju:nifaid] adj. 统一的；一致标准的
descent [di'sent] n. 下降；血统；袭击
atmosphere ['ætməsfiə] n. 气氛；大气；空气
confines ['kɔnfainz] vt. 限制；禁闭
biology [bai'ɔlədʒi] n. （一个地区全部的）生物；生物学
functions ['fʌnkʃənz] n. 功能；函数（function 的复数形式）
entity ['entiti] n. 实体；存在；本质
intention [in'tenʃ(ə)n] n. 意图；目的；意向；愈合
inexpensive [inik'spensiv; inek-] adj. 便宜的
heerleading ['tʃiə,li:diŋ] n. 带领啦啦队
cheering ['tʃiəriŋ] adj. 令人高兴的
spirit ['spirit] n. 精神；心灵；情绪；志气
tight-knit adj. 亲密的，紧密的
enthusiastic [in,θju:zi'æstik; en-] adj. 热情的；热心的；狂热的
tenants ['tenənts] n. 承租人；房客；佃户；居住者
fellowship ['felə(ʊ)ʃip] n. 友谊；奖学金；研究员职位
ecology [i'kɔlədʒi; e-] n. 生态学；社会生态学
economics [i:kə'nɔmiks; ek-] n. 经济学；国家的经济状况
volunteer [,vɔlən'tiə] n. 志愿者；志愿兵
geography [dʒi'ɔgrəfi] n. 地理；地形
charity ['tʃæriti] n. 慈善；施舍；慈善团体
kayaking ['kaiækiŋ] n. 划独木舟
canoeing [kə'nu:iŋ] n. 乘独木舟
rafting [ra:ftiŋ] n. 乘筏
choreography [,kɔri'ɔgrəfə] n. 编舞
intramural [,intrə'mjʊrəl] adj. 校内的，内部的
pursuing [pə'sju:iŋ] n. 继续；从事；追赶；纠缠

physics ['fɪzɪks] n. 物理学；物理现象

sociology [,səʊsɪ'ɒlədʒɪ, -ʃɪ-] n. 社会学；[生]群体生态学

anthropology [,ænθrə'pɒlədʒɪ] n. 人类学

forum ['fɔːrəm] n. 论坛，讨论会；法庭；公开讨论的广场

disciplines ['dɪsɪplɪns] n. 学科；纪律；训练；惩罚

bond [bɒnd] vi. 结合，团结在一起

preventable [prɪ'vɛntəbl] adj. 可预防的；可阻止的；可防止的

fundraiser ['fʌnd,reɪzə] n. 资金筹集人；资金筹集活动

advocate ['ædvəkət] vt. 提倡，主张，拥护

vegetarians [,vedʒɪ'tɛərɪəns] n. 素食者；食草动物

vegans ['viːg(ə)ns] n. （英）严格的素食主义者

collegiate [kə'liːdʒ(i)ət] adj. 大学的；学院的；大学生的

intramural [,ɪntrə'mjʊərəl] adj. 校内的，内部的

seriously ['sɪərɪəslɪ] adv. 认真地；严重地，严肃地

chess [tʃes] n. 国际象棋，西洋棋

passion ['pæʃ(ə)n] n. 激情；热情；酷爱；盛怒

alerting [ə'lɜːtɪŋ] v. 报警；发信号（alert 的 ing 形式）

Conversation Questions

Are you involved in any clubs at your school?

If you could join a club at school, which one would you join?

How important is it for you to be a member of a club?

Would you like to be in charge of the club or just a member? Why?

If you are a member of a club, is there anything about the club that you would change? Explain why.

Do you have time to be in a club?

Will being in a club help you in the real world?

What are some things you can learn by being in a club?

Do you know of any international clubs?

Would you encourage your friends to join a club? Why?

Discussion Questions

Are you organized enough to do your studying and attend club meetings?

As a student, how important is it to be a club member?

Do you ever wish you could join clubs at your school now?

Tell me about one of the clubs you are in.

What is the most important part about being in a club?

Practice Dialogues

Throughout this book you will have a variety of dialogues that you can use to practice speaking and asking questions. Each section of the book will have 3 dialogues for your use.

Dialogue # 1 – 2 Students

A: So, are you going to join any clubs this year?

B: I'm not sure. I've never been in a club before.

A: Really?

B: Yes, at my former school we had no time for clubs.

A: Well, that will change. What interests do you have?

B: Well, I like photography, swimming and reading.

A: Okay. There is a photography club forming on Tuesdays at 6pm in the library. The sign says anyone can join.

B: That sounds good. And it is after my late class on Tuesdays and I would still have time for dinner.

A: Here's one about swimming. They call themselves the Swimeroos. What a silly name!

B: What does it say about swimming?

A: They meet at the gym on Wednesdays at 6:30pm. They participate in local swimming competitions with other colleges and universities. They are part of the Intramural Program. It also says it is co-ed.

B: Hmmm. Competitions? I'm not too sure about that one.

A: You don't have to compete to be in the club. The people that go are there to swim and have fun. If some are more competitive than the others, they can do the competition. I think you should give it a try.

B: Well, I do love to swim. And it would be good to meet more people on campus. Okay, you talked me into it.

A: I see a sign for the Literary Guild. They meet every other Thursday at 7pm. in the library. This group discusses the latest works being published today. That sounds interesting. I might even join that group.

B: Great. We can both join then.

Dialogue #2 – Student and Professor

S: I came in to speak to you about the Literary Guild.

P: Yes, what would you like to know?

S: Well, I enjoy reading a great deal, but I also enjoy writing. I have

been writing poetry for 4 years now and I want to know if there is a Poetry Club on campus?

P: Well, there is no Poetry Club on campus, but that doesn't mean we can't start one.

S: Well, how would we start a new club?

P: You would need to go to the Student Government Association and get a form for a new club.

S: Okay. Then what do I do? Fill it out?

P: yes, and no. Eventually you will fill out the form, but there are a few others things you need to do as well.

S: Such as?

P: You need to have at least 15 students sign up to begin the club. You need to find a space in which you can hold meetings. You need to elect officers to run the club and you need to get an academic advisor to supervise the club.

S: Gosh, that's a lot of stuff just to open a new club.

P: If you are passionate about your poetry and you want to share it with others, you need to decide if the paperwork and legwork is worth it.

S: I think it is. However, I do not know of an academic advisor who would be willing to supervise the club.

P: Luckily for you, you are speaking to a poet. I would be happy to be the advisor for the club.

S: Really? Wonderful! Well, I will go and get the form and get everything done within this week. Is that okay with you?

P: That would be fine. When you have all the students signed up, bring everything to my office. I will look over everything and then we will start the Poetry Club.

Dialogue #3 – 2 Students

A: I have a full schedule this semester.

B: Really? How many credits are you taking?

A: 18 credits plus 2 labs.

B: Wow! That's 20 credits in total. You must be really organized.

A: Well, I like to stay busy. I don't enjoy having idle time.

B: Most students would be just the opposite....they only want a few classes and more time to sleep or play computer games.

A: I was taught to keep active, so that is what I am doing.

B: What do you do in your spare time?

A: I have a few clubs that I belong to.

B: You have time to be in clubs?

A: Sure. I have a system when it comes to homework, and after it is completed, I have time to go to my clubs.

B: I see. What clubs are you in?

A: I am in the Biology Club, Poetry Club and Swimming Club.

B: I am amazed. I am taking 15 credits this semester and I barely have time to finish my studies and have dinner. How do you do it?

A: It all depends on how organized you are and how disciplined you are.

B: Meaning?

A: For me, club activities do not happen if I have a research paper or big exam to study for. Class work always comes first. I use the clubs as a bonus for finishing my tasks.

B: Oh, sort of like a reward for good behavior or for making good grades.

A: Yes, exactly.

B: So, can you help me get myself organized?

A: Of course. It is not difficult to do, but you must be willing to make some compromises as you go along.

B: Okay. I can compromise on anything as long as I have better grades.

A: Great. Let's get started.

B: Okay.

Chapter 2
Getting Around the City or Town

熟悉新地方

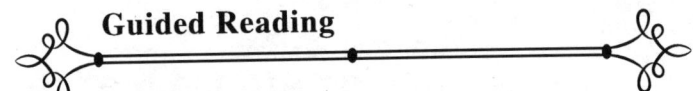
Guided Reading

当你在陌生的国度将行李安顿下来后,该出门转转了。初来乍到,熟悉情况很重要。如何能在陌生的地方不至迷路?第一次出门熟悉环境应随身携带哪些物品呢?让我们一起来check一下吧!

After you get your bearings on campus and you know where everything is located, it is time to branch out and see the town, city or country. For the first few excursions, you should use the buddy system: pick someone to go along with you just in case you get lost or something happens to you. To be on the safe side, there are some things you can take along to make your first trip special and memorable:

1.Bring a camera – You can take pictures to send back home to show your parents you are alive and well. You can keep them to remember your first visit to the city and they are pictures of you and your new friend.

2.Phone numbers – In most western countries you are not required to carry your passport with you when you are out sightseeing or even shopping. However, it is always good to bring your college identification with you. This has your name on it, a picture of you and in most places it can be used when you are asked for identification. Most places would rather see a driver's license, but if you do not drive, this will be just as handy. In addition to carrying your id you should also have a short list of telephone numbers just in case something bad happens. Always include your RA on your list. Other people to include would be your parents, best friends and a contact person at school (not the RA). If you have a medical problem or a history of allergies, you should have them listed on your phone list too. Sometimes we want to try the local food and we end up getting sick from it. Better to be safe than sorry.

3.Backpack or Rucksack – Many students when viewing a town, city or the country for the first time always find something to buy and take back to the school with them. The best thing to bring along on your trip is a backpack or a rucksack. You can put all of the things you wish to carry in it and just sling it over your back. It is a safer way to carry valuables without

losing them.

4.Map – Even if your companion is a local native, it is always good to bring a map. This will help you to adjust to your surroundings. When you get to any destination, sit for a few minutes and look at the map to see exactly where you are. Your friend can easily show you on the map and this would be a great way to learn about the places you are visiting, but also give you an opportunity to get to know your friend better. Later when you venture out on your own, having the map will be useful just in case you get lost.

出国必带或必买物品表

常用物品分类	细分
文件类	机票车票，护照，身份证，录取通知书，当地指南手册，地图，地址电话通讯册
小用具	手机，笔记本电脑，相机，胶卷，随身听，闹钟，手电筒，刮胡刀，计算器，电池，指甲刀，开罐器，小型电热杯，小型衣架，针线包，吹风机，纸笔
穿戴类	备换服装，备换鞋，睡衣，领带围巾，帽子，手套，泳衣，短裤，生理用品，毛巾，化妆品，防晒霜，饰品，洗浴用品，梳子，牙刷牙膏
饮食	必要的药品，饮料，食品。吃不惯国外食品的可多带保存时间较长的国内食品

出门应该坐什么车呢？坐公交、打车是否也能像在国内一样容易呢？留学目的地的地理位置也至关重要，不仅仅因为交通便利，人文差别也十分重要哦！

There are many modes of transportation when you are in a western country. Depending on the town or city, the mode of transportation is up to you. In large cities people usually take the bus or subway. They seldom take a taxi because of the cost. Taxis cost much more than the bus or subway. As a new arrival, you might want to try the bus. Most bus drivers will be happy to point you in the right direction if there is a particular place you wish to see. On the subway people are not as friendly. They are on the subway trying to get home or to work. They are usually not in the mood to talk to a stranger. The fastest way to get to your destination is by taxi, but it will cost you. So be aware of the costs before you decide which mode you wish to use.

When you decide to study abroad, one aspect of your journey that you must pay close attention to is location. For example, in the southern parts of the United States, people tend to be very friendly and hospitable. They would treat you like they would treat a neighbor and even a relative, always kind and willing to talk about anything. However, in the northern parts of the country the people are less friendly or trusting. It is very difficult to engage them in conversation or to even get directions from them. They simply do not care about other people. Since you will be living on a university campus, or close to one, you will find the students and staff to be friendly and helpful. It does not matter where you are located in the country, the population or community at the university is diverse and everyone will be quite helpful. Your only concerns will be when you are not on campus trying to find your way around. So location in a country is quite important for any student wishing to study abroad.

Human beings are creatures of habit. When we do something or go somewhere, we always end up going back to the same places and doing the same things. As a new student in a foreign country, do not try to reinvent yourself. Do things that you would normally do back in your country and try new things when you have a group of friends with you. Attempting to try

something new by yourself might cause some problems for you. It would be better if you had some friends around to help you if something goes wrong. Traveling around a new city can be very exciting, but it can also make you quite nervous. The first few times you travel into the city, take a friend or two along. It is always a good idea to travel with someone. As mentioned earlier, a notebook in the city is quite useful. You can write down addresses of places you have visited in case you want to return to them. You can write down a few details about your trip and how you felt. Later you can relay these feelings in an email to your friends and family back home.

There are a few things you should know about the city: where the nearest hospital is located, where Chinatown is located and where the best shopping areas are located. Obviously, it is important to know where the local hospital is in the city. If you can't get into the clinic on campus, you can go to the hospital. Most of the major cities in the US have a section of the city called Chinatown. Chinatown is primarily the home of Chinese-Americans or Chinese immigrants. The food is authentic Chinese cuisine. The language is usually Mandarin with some English too. The whole atmosphere of Chinatown is similar to parts of Beijing or Shanghai. Small shops, dumplings, Peking duck and many other delicacies from the mainland await you. If you ever feel homesick, plan to see Chinatown with your new friends and teach them a few things about Chinese food. You will enjoy it and they will, too.

As a student, you should be made aware of the shopping places that most students frequent. Most university students are on budgets; this means they do not spend a lot of money on clothes, so they are always looking for bargains.

If your roommates ask you to come along for a day of shopping, go ahead. You might find some interesting items at low prices.

Depending on where you are located in the country, asking and getting directions might be difficult. If you are on campus and you need directions to a place off campus, ask the RA. He/she would know where you want to go. The RAs are usually local people and they know the city. If you can get directions prior to leaving the campus, you will have an easier time traveling. Asking people in the public for directions is a different matter. We said that northern people tend to be cautious and unfriendly. They would rather not talk about anything especially to a stranger. However, if you are in the north and you need directions, the best places to get directions are at the police station, post office or doctor's office. The people working in these facilities tend to be very helpful and regardless of how the rest of the citizens behave, they are more outgoing and friendly. They will not give you wrong directions, but a person on the street might.

In the southern part of the US, you would have no trouble getting directions. The southern people are quite friendly and talkative. The best place to get directions would be a local restaurant, drug store, bank or post office. Even the local police station or fire department would give good advice to you.

A few notes about being in the city:

1. If you are female, carry your purse or backpack in the front against your chest, especially if you are in a metropolitan area. Many people have had their purses stolen very quickly by someone going in the opposite direction. Keeping it close to your body will make it more difficult for someone to take it.

2. In a restaurant it is customary to tip the waiter or waitress. The usual

amount to tip is 20% of the total bill. The best way to figure out how much to tip is to look at your bill, locate the tax on the bill and multiply the tax by 20. Simply leave the money on the table when you get up to go or if you wish you can hand it to the waiter/waitress personally and say thank you.

3. If you find yourself walking down the street alone and someone is walking toward you, cross to the other side of the street before you get too close to the person. If they also cross the street, turn around and go the other way or step into a store until the person has passed by. Never assume that the person coming towards you is friendly. It is better to be safe than sorry.

4. Make sure you know the travel times for buses and subways so you are not stuck in the city overnight.

5. Always keep spare change in your purse/wallet in case you need to make a phone call.

6. If you are a male student, think about putting your wallet in your front pants pocket while in the city. It is an easy target for a pick-pocket if you leave it in the back. Don't take any chances, be smart.

Helpful Hints

Students going abroad have a tendency to trust people, especially when they are asking for directions. Be cautious! There are some things you can do to make your trip to the city better for you. Tell someone at the university where you are going and what time you should be coming back. You can tell the RA or even your roommate. If you are not back by a certain time, it is best that you call and inform someone that you will be late.

各国交通状况：

美国：

美国交通方便，最基本的交通工具是飞机和汽车，铁路也很发达，一些大城市的地铁四通八达。美国的长途巴士因其快捷、舒适、价廉而很受欢迎,长途汽车公司有好几家,路线最广的是灰狗长途汽车公司(Grey hould),除美国国内各地外,还可通到加拿大。

美国铁路 Amtrak 是公私合营的公司,干线长达四万多公里。

注意事项:搭乘公共交通车辆要注意自己的钱物,留心车内的动静,如发现异常赶快告诉司机处理,自己不要随便介入。等车时要和其他搭客站在一起,不要太靠近地铁站台或马路,以保证安全。如果是夜晚,一定要在灯光明亮和有人的地方等车。

英国:

英国是欧洲使用汽车最多的国家,87%的公路旅程由小汽车完成,只有12%由公共汽车完成。英国交通的一个最大特点是没有人车混合交通,城市中主要为机动车辆交通,基本没有自行车道。各个城市以及城市与城市之间的公路都设有固定或可变的交通标识、指示和信号灯,道路语言比较系统和完善。任何路口都设有无论夜晚还是白天都清晰可辨的指路牌,指向相连的道路和街区。车流容易汇聚和交叉的地方,都有禁行或让路的标志,必须严格恪守,否则,出现交通事故必须自己承担责任。

以英国首都伦敦为例,从100多年前把发展城市立体交通作为一项战略性措施实施后至今,伦敦已建成包括地铁、轻轨、公共汽车和出租车为一体,方便快捷的交通网络。伦敦交通的70%依靠地铁,每小时发出的列车达90班次。地铁线路纵横交错,十几条不同的线路贯穿东南西北,与火车路路相连,一到六区,地上地下火车来往穿梭,仅在伦敦市中心就有七八个火车站。地面公共交通也不断发展,整个城市数百路公共汽车,伦敦人自己也说不清准确数字。

英国跟中国交通最大的区别是靠左行驶哦!

澳大利亚各大城市的交通工具,包括日常交通工具和旅游交通工具同国内各大城市基本相同,其中除了出租车以外,对于其他日常交通工具,学生均可凭学生

证享受优惠价。大致可以分为以下几类：

1. 自行车

在校园内，自行车始终是最便利的交通工具，但即使在澳洲，你也需要为你的自行车配备一个良好的车锁。另外，根据澳洲法律规定，骑车人必须配备自行车专用头盔且必须在人行道上行驶，不得驶入机动车道。墨尔本是骑车游览的好地方，该市路面相对平坦，并有设计好的大都市区骑车游览路线。其中有两条路线最佳，一条是绕菲利浦湾港岸边，从墨尔本港（Port Melbourne）到布莱顿（Brighton）的自行车路线，另一条是沿亚拉河（Yarra River），从市区出行20多公里的自行车路线。

2. 公共汽车和有轨电车

公共汽车是最常见的出行工具。澳洲的公共汽车按段收费，除了直接向司机购票以外还可以选择各类"十次卡"。另外需要注意的是，搭乘澳洲的公共汽车，下车需预先提示司机，如无提示司机有权不停靠车站。澳洲的公共汽车有人数限制，尤其注意在公共交通工具上逃票会涉及个人信用记录。罚款 A$100/次。

3. 火车和轻轨

悉尼-拥有巨大的郊区铁路网络和密集的班次，使火车远比公共汽车快捷。火车大约早上5点开班，午夜收班。另外，单轨铁路和城市轻轨是市中心出行的很好途径。单轨铁路环绕达伶港(Darling Harbour)，将其与市中心连接起来。城市轻轨经过达伶港与唐人街(China Town)，在中央火车站与派蒙区（Pyrmont）之间每天造词24小时开行。

4. 出租车

澳大利亚的出租汽车车身以黄色为主，都安装石油液化器装置，引擎盖上喷漆大大的 TAXI。除此以外，车身上喷的文字图案较多，如公司徽图、叫车电话号码、车辆牌照号码等。街上出租车虽然不少，但要像国内一样"招手即停"却难以办到。定点上车是这儿的规矩。

在澳洲留学要记住，在澳洲行人、车辆皆遵守左侧通行的原则，这跟中国正相反。

加拿大

作为一个拥有高水平生活质量的发达国家，加拿大的交通可谓四通八达。中国留学生在初到加拿大时，往往因对当地交通不熟悉吃了不少苦头。所谓"千里之行，始于足下"，只有在对交通状况有所了解的情况下，外出时方可有备无患顺利出行。相对而言加拿大在各种交通设施名称上也是有所不同的。

Bus：公共汽车是所有城市利用的即干净又安静的交通手段。连接城市的各个角落和没有地铁和其他交通手段的地区，细心安排 Bus 和 Bus 之间的换车的区间，使各路线之间都连接起来。加拿大 Bus Net work 被称为 LRT(Light-Rapid-Transit) System。需要注意的是，渥太华的公交车以颜色区分，黑色路线全天运行，红色路线只在平日的高峰时间运行，绿色快速线在平日的高峰时间运行，票价为 3.5 加元；蓝色线仅在早晨 6 点以前运行。

Subway：加拿大的地铁并非都在地下，称呼也不一样。蒙特利尔的地铁在地表以下，而且还很深。由于建造比较早，地铁运营得还很不错。蒙特利尔的地铁叫 Metro。如果你看到了有 Metro 的标记，那就是地铁站。在蒙特利尔千万不要用 subway 这个词来打听地铁在哪里。不然，热心的人会详细地告诉你 subway 在哪个地方。当你到了 subway 门前，你才恍然地看到 subway 连锁快餐店的招牌。多伦多的地铁才真正地称为 subway，大部分的路段是在地下运行。由于多伦多面积大，地铁跨度也长，因此特别是绿线和黄线地铁使用率很高。因出行需要可办理 1 个月为单位的 Monthly Pass，这样即省钱有方便。它的优点是不管次数和交通工具，1 日到 30 日随便利用。

Sky Train

sky train 如同上海的高架公路一样是在高架铁路上运行，被称为"空中列车"。 Sky Train 连接温哥华的 Vancouver Downtown 和 Burnaby，星期一到星期五是从早晨 5：50 分到半夜 1：17 分，星期六是从早晨 6：15 到半夜 1：17 分运营，星期日是从早晨 8：47 分到半夜 12：17 分运行。这个时间表是和换乘 bus 的时间是有联系的，它的始发站是 Waterfront。

Street Car

Street Car 被称为"有轨列车"是多伦多的独特的交通手段,现在只有北美地区的几个城市才具备。连接 St.Clair Ave, College,Dundas,Queen,King Streets 地区的东西方向。

Sea Bus

"海上巴士"连接温哥华 Downtown 的 Waterfront 站和 North Vancourer 的 Lonsdale Quay。每 15 分钟发一次,需要的时间是 12 分钟左右,可以欣赏城市美丽的 Skyline 和港口的景色。

Taxi

出租车在加拿大随处可见,招手即停。出租车公司名单列于黄页电话簿 Taxi cabs 栏内,可以按黄页打电话给出租汽车公司叫车,或者提前预约,出租车可按照约定的时间地点等候。除了车内计价器上显示的车费外,一般还要另给小费(约为车费的 10%～15%)。

C-Train

卡尔加里 C-Train 轻轨系统是在主要干道的中间运行,并因此得名。是北美洲第一个轻铁系统,总长 42.1km,设有 2 条主要在地面营运路线(201 及 202),由市营的卡尔加里运输营运。

此外在加拿大行人有优先的路权。很多路口的灯杆上都有为行人专门设置的按钮,按下按钮,信号灯会转变让行人得到优先通过权。有些路口同时配有声音提示,在没有红绿信号灯的小路口,都有"停止"的标示,依照加拿大的交通规则,机动车看到这样的标识,都应优先停车。在加拿大,如果司机违规,罚款很是严厉的动辄罚款 1000 美元。

Vocabulary

bearings ['beriŋz] n. 行李

branch out 扩大活动范围

excursion [ik'skə:ʃən] n. 短途旅游

buddy ['bʌdi:] n. 伙伴

memorable ['memə:əbəl] adj. 难忘的

allergy ['ælədʒi] n. 过敏

rucksack ['rʌksæk] n. 帆布背包

valuables ['væljəbəlz] n. 珍贵物品

companion [kəm'pænyən] n. 同伴

destination [destə'neiʃən] n. 目的地

mode ['məud] n. 方式

seldom ['seldəm] adv. 极难得

arrival [ə'raivəl] n. 到达

aspect ['æ,spekt] n. 方面

southern ['səðə:n] adj. 在南方的；向南方的；朝南方的

hospitable ['hɔ'spitəbəl] adj. 好客的，殷勤的

northern ['nɔ:rðə:n] adj. 北方的，北部的

diverse [dai'və:s] adj. 多样的；相异的

tendency ['tendənsi:] n. 趋势，趋向

cautious ['kɔ:ʃəs] adj. 小心的，谨慎的

purse ['pə:s] n.（尤指女用）小钱包

briefcase ['bri:,fkeis] n. 公文包

steal ['sti:l] v. 偷盗，窃取

surroundings [sə:'aundiŋz] n. 周围的事物；环境

watchful ['wɔtʃfəl] adj. 警惕的，注意的

accustomed [ə'kəstəmd] adj. 惯常的，通常的

overly ['əuvə:li:] adv. 过度地

creatures ['kri:tʃəz] n. 生物，动物（creature 的名词复数）；人

habit ['hæbit] n. 习惯，习性；气质

reinvent [ˌriːin'vent] vt. （在不知他人以发明的情况下）重复发明，彻底改造，重新使用

nervous ['nəːvəs] adj. 神经的；紧张不安的；

relay ['riːlei] n. 接替人员，替班；传递；接力赛；继电器　vt. 转播，传达；用驿马递送，使接替；分程传递

obviously ['ɔbviəsli] adv. 明显地

primarily ['praimərili] adv. 首先；首要地，主要地；根本上；本来

immigrants ['imigrənts] n. 移民（immigrant 的名词复数）

authentic [ɔː'θentik] adj. 真的，真正的；可信的，可靠的

atmosphere ['ætməsfiə] n. 大气，空气；大气层；风格，基调；气氛

delicacies ['delikəsiːz] n. 棘手（delicacy 的名词复数）；精致；精美的食物

mainland ['meinlənd] n. 大陆；本土　adj. 大陆的；本土的

await [ə'weit] vt. 等候；等待；期待

budgets ['bʌdʒits] n. 预算（budget 的名词复数）；预算案；预算拨款；一束

bargains ['baːginz] n. 协议，交易（bargain 的名词复数）；特价商品 v. 讨价还价，商谈（bargain 的第三人称单数）；提出条件，要求得到

unfriendly [ʌn'frendliː] adj. 不友好的，有敌意的；冷漠的；不利的；（气候）不宜人的

especially [is'peʃəli] adv. 尤其地；主要地，格外地；显著地；异常地

stranger ['streindʒə] n. 陌生人，不认识的人；外地人；局外人；门外汉　adj. 不熟悉的，陌生的 (strange) 的比较级

regardless [ri'gaːdlis] adv. 不管怎样，无论如何；不惜费用地　adj. 不重视的，不尊敬的；不顾虑的，不关心的；不受注意的

citizens ['sItIzənz] n. 公民（citizen 的名词复数）；国民，市民，平民

behave [bi'heiv] vi. 表现；举止端正；自然反应　vt. 使守规矩

outgoing ['aʊtˌgəʊiŋ] adj. 对人友好的，开朗的；出发的，外出的；即将离职的

talkative ['tɔ:kətiv] adj. 健谈的，多嘴的，喜欢说话的

metropolitan [ˌmetrə'pɔlitən] adj. 大都会的；大城市的； n. 大城市人

customary ['kʌstəməri] adj. 习惯的；通常的；照惯例的 n. 习惯法；风俗志

waiter ['weitə] n. 侍者；服务员；托盘

waitress ['weitris] n. 女服务员；女侍者

tax [tæks] n. 税，税额；负担

personally ['pɜ:sənəli] adv. 亲自地；就个人而言；个别地；私人地（与工作相对）

assume [ə'sju:m] vt. 假设，假定；呈现

stuck [stʌk] v. 刺 (stick 的过去式及过去分词) adj. 动不了的；被卡住的；被…缠住的；被…难住的，不知所措

overnight [ˌəʊvə'nait] adv. 在晚上；在夜里；突然，很快 adj. 一整夜的；晚上的；突然的；很快的 n. 前一天的晚上；一夜的逗留 vi. 过一夜

wallet ['wɔlit] n. 钱包，皮夹子

pants [pænts] n. <英>（紧身的）短裤；<美>裤子

pocket ['pɔkit] n. 口袋，钱袋

pick-pocket [pik 'pɔkit] n. 扒手

Conversation Questions

Do you like to travel?
Will it be hard to travel in another country?
If you could travel anywhere in the world, where would you go?
Are you afraid of traveling alone?

What do you need before traveling to another country?
What is the most interesting place you have visited?
What place would you like to visit? Why?
What is your favorite mode of travel?
How many times have you traveled abroad?
Do you think you will stay on campus more or travel more? Why?

Discussion Questions

How difficult is it for you to ask people for directions?
Would you go out and see the city be yourself or with a friend? Why?
What sort of problems would a stranger face in a new city?
Can you ask for directions?
Tell me the most important information you know about yourself if you get lost in a new place.
Do you think being in a large city in a western country would be different than a large city in China? Why?
Can you read a map?
What would you do the first day you are in a new city?
Explain how you would feel seeing a new town, city or country for the first time.
If you were in a large city in the United States, would you like to visit China Town? Why?

让我们选择好留学目的地

"我喜欢英国,泰晤士河两岸古老的宫殿与钟楼,坍圮的城堡与斑驳的外墙时刻对过往行人诉说这日不落帝国往昔的荣耀。""美国集中了世界上最顶尖的大学群,有着平等、开放、自由的学习环境,这是我选择美国最主要的原因。"……

说起留学目的地,有的学生已心有所属,但很多同学和家长对于如何选择留学目的地尚存在疑惑。经常听家长这样问:你觉得孩子该去哪儿好?其他孩子都去哪儿留学?这是许许多多留学生家长们最想知道但又最困惑的问题。让我们一起来倾听留学生们讲述自己的留学体验,你或许能从中获得启发,确定自己的目标。

英国

出镜人物:黄小明目前就读于英国伯明翰大学,虽然英国国土面积有限,可离开城市后仍然可以体会到旷野对心灵的触碰:浓郁的绿色,几乎触手可及的白云与悠闲的牛群和马匹。小镇里,如果你在市区十字路口多晃悠几圈,说不定就会有个挂着拐杖的老奶奶或老爷爷颤颤巍巍地问你:"Are you lost?"超市里买东西时,收银员会热情地称呼你"sunshine"。

在英国上学,教授和老师有时候会超乎想象地热情,一旦他打开话匣子,你就埋怨自己早饭没有再吃一个三明治。

在英国有 180 多所高校,设有 14000 多个专业和 37000 个学位,教育历史的悠久和教育质量的国家认可度家喻户晓。英国受到很多学生欢迎的原因除了教育质量和名校口碑外最重要的是英语的语言优势,作为世界通用语言和使用最广泛的语言的优势。

俄罗斯

出镜人物:黄天曾在俄罗斯留学,现已回国。俄罗斯重视发展文化事业,大量出版图书和报刊,建立了许多图书馆、博物馆、文化馆、俱乐部等群众性文化设施。冬宫和俄罗斯国家博物馆很近,每次遇到节日都可以去逛,拿着学生证就全都免费了。

俄罗斯重视对博物馆珍品和历史建筑文物的保护,建国以来扩建和新建了许多博物馆,在很多博物馆里随时都有坐在角落的老人耐心地给你讲解其中的故事,博物馆里还有很多老师带着学生来参观,有的小孩还不到 10 岁,也都来接受艺术

的熏陶。

俄罗斯的世界知名大学很多。比如圣彼得堡的列宾美术学院，就是世界上最著名的四大美术学院之一，"盛产"知名画家。巴甫洛夫国立医科大学，是俄罗斯第一流的医科大学，排名欧洲最好的医科大学的前十位。俄罗斯大学学费相对比较低，赴俄签证办理起来也很快。但是俄罗斯的治安比起欧美国家要差许多。

美国

出镜人物：李晴目前就读于美国纽约的一所高中在美国课堂上，老师总要腾出至少15分钟的时间要求学生提问题，在座的学生会连珠炮似地发问。你可以在课堂上和老师争得面红耳赤，老师会给你很高的分，并且鼓励你和他讨论。

世界排名前100位的大学中约有50%为美国的大学，美国在2005年对中国开放学生签证，美国中学教育展在2007年首次登陆中国，相较于其他国家而言，美国的校园中语言环境更加纯正。

美国是一个开放且包容的国家，每个学校都会招收一定比例的、不同地域和种族的学生，他们带来了多元的文化，更带来了丰富的理念，这些为学生了解世界不同文化提供了一个很好的平台。另外以现有汇率计算，以赴美留学四年修完学士学位为例，留学美国的平均成本要比以往便宜不少。

Practice Dialogues

Throughout this book you will have a variety of dialogues that you can use to practice speaking and asking questions. Each section of the book will have 3 dialogues for your use.

Dialogue # 1 – 2 Students

A: Would you like to go downtown with me this afternoon?

B: Sure, what time do you want to go?

A: Well, I was thinking of going after my English class, around 2 o'clock.

B: That's sounds good. I have a math class that finishes at 1:45.

A: Great. Let's meet back at the dorm and then go from there.

B: Okay. I will be ready when you get back from class.

A: Oh, make sure you wear sports shoes.

B: Why?

A: Because we will be doing a lot of walking.

B: Good. I enjoy walking.

A: And I will show you some of the city. I will be your guide.

B: That sounds like fun. Can I bring my camera along?

A: Sure. I can take you to some very famous sites and you can have your picture taken there.

B: I would like that. I want to send some home to my parents and friends.

A: No problem. So, I will see you here at 2pm.

B: Sounds great. See you then.

A: Bye

B: Bye, have fun in English.

Dialogue #2 – Same 2 Students

A: See that building? It was built 300 years ago. It is one of the oldest buildings in America.

B: Hmmm. 300 years is not really that old.

A: Well, if you think about it, America is not an old country, so 300 years in a young country seems old.

B: I guess you are right. In China, we see old buildings all the time. We have a history that goes back over 5,000 years.

A: Wow! Did you have to study the history of China when you were growing up?

B: Yes, we did have some classes about history.

A: That's a lot of information to study. I'm glad I never had to do that.

B: The history of China is so long, that most schools only look at the dynasties and the history of their region. China is too large for anyone to remember all the history that happened around the country.

A: That makes sense. In America we are required to study our state history, and students who major in history take classes that cover all of American history.

B: What is that over there?

A: That is one of our most famous sites. Let's get off the bus and go see it.

B: Okay, you go first, I will follow you.

A: This is the Metropolitan Museum of Modern Art. Inside are famous pieces of art, sculpture and even manuscripts from famous artists around the world.

B: Oh I love art. Shall we go inside?

A: Sure. Are you ready?

B: Yes.

A: Oh, before we go inside, there are some areas where you are not allowed to take a picture. The flash of the camera might damage the paintings. There are signs posted. You'll see.

B: Thanks for telling me beforehand.

A: Let's go.

B: Okay.

A: We are in luck. They have the Mona Lisa on display this month. It was brought over from France.

B: The REAL Mona Lisa?

A: Yep. This museum is one of the best in the world. It ranks at the top with the Louvre in Paris.

B: Wow!

A: Shall we go see her?

B: Yes, please. I want to say that I actually looked at Mona Lisa.

A: This way.

Dialogue #3 – Student and RA

RA: I heard you went to the museum today. Did you like it?

S: Oh yes, it was really exciting.

RA: What part did you like the most?

S: I would have to say that looking at the Mona Lisa was the best part.

RA: Really? When I saw it I was disappointed.

S: Why? It is such a masterpiece.

RA: Yes, but I had to wait in line for such a long time and when I finally got up to see it, it was locked behind a wall and I had to look in that little hole of glass to see it.

S: Now that you mention it, I did stand a while to see it. I was a little disappointed because it wasn't just there hanging on the wall. But thinking

back on the day, it was the highlight.

RA: Did you get any pictures?

S: Oh yes, I have a ton of pictures to download and send back home.

RA: Good. Make sure you take lots of pictures when you are in the city.

S: Why is that?

RA: Well, you never know who you might meet. It could be a movie star or some important politician.

S: Have you ever met a movie star?

RA: Not personally, but I've seen a few having dinner or walking in the street.

S: That must have been exciting for you.

RA: Yes, it was, but I did not have my camera with me, so I couldn't take a picture. Besides, they have their pictures taken all the time.

S: Well they are starts, so they should be used to that.

RA: Sure, but I think they also like to have privacy.

S: That makes sense; being in front of a camera, making a movie for others to enjoy. I guess they would like some private time without pictures being taken.

RA: Well, just make sure you always have your camera with you so you can get some good pictures for your parents and friends to see in China.

S: I will.

RA: Time for me to do some studying. Have a good evening.

S: Thanks, time for me to study also. Good night.

RA: Good night.

Chapter 3
Dining Out

外出就餐

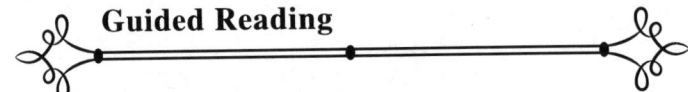

Guided Reading

看书累了吗？想不想享用一份大餐好好犒劳一下自己？还没有在校外用过餐？那可不行，国外大学生活可不仅仅是学习，在外用餐也是体验西方文化的一部分。如何选择用餐的地点，什么时间到餐馆合适，去之前可要好好规划一下啊。让我们一起来看看下面的就餐指南吧！

As a student at a university or college in the United States, the majority of your time is spent on campus eating at the dining halls or cafeterias available to you. However, there will be times when you and your friends will want to have a change of pace and the best way to make that happen is to experience a new restaurant. If you are not sure what type of food you wish to eat, simply ask some of the students for suggestions. They can tell you all you need to know about the restaurants in the area.

Many foreign students come to the US to get a good education and while they are studying and accomplishing their own goals, they sometimes think they should never venture outside of the campus unless it is absolutely necessary. The old saying, 'variety is the spice of life', is something you should use while in the United States. Go out and see what is around you. Experience all that America offer. The more you do and see, the more stories you can tell when you return to China. In order to do this and do it successfully, you need to follow a few simple guidelines. These are not rules; they are thoughts that will help you when you decide to go out for a nice dinner away from the campus.

Never go alone. 不要单独外出。

You should always plan a dinner with at least one friend. This is merely common sense. If you get lost, you can easily ask for directions. However, if you get hurt you will need someone to help you. Besides, no one likes to eat alone. So, get a few friends together and have a great time.

Find a suitable location. 找个合适的地点。

When choosing a restaurant, remember that you xusually have to rely on public transportation (bus, taxi, subway) to get to and leave the restaurant. If one of your friends has a car, then the location of the restaurant depends on how long you want to travel to get there. In most

cases, it is wise to find something within an hour travel time from the campus. If you are not sure, ask your RA and he/she can give you good advice about restaurants in the area.

Budget. 做好预算。

College students are very good at finding restaurants that do not cost much. They ask around the school and someone will mention a place that has great food and a reasonable price. Once this information is obtained, the dinner plans start to come into focus. Remember that you are a college student and you need to be conservative with your money. It is a wise move for you to be frugal or thrifty when it comes to food. One reason for being frugal or thrifty is that if you are not, others will try to take advantage of you. They will try to get you to pay for them and they will thank you so much for doing it. Unfortunately, they will not stop at one time. If they know you have money, they will try to convince you to buy them other things like clothes, electronics, or even pay for trips. So don't let anyone know that you have a lot of money with you. This could prove dangerous if you are in a large city. Play it safe and carry your money in front poket, so no one can take it from you.

Time. 计划好时间。

Being a student you must have a schedule. It is important to maintain that schedule so you can be successful in school. With that in mind, one of the things you need to look at when choosing a restaurant is time. This is not about how far the restaurant is from the school, but about how long it takes for your food to arrive at your table, how long it takes to stand in line before being seated, etc. You need to ask yourself if you want to go to a restaurant that is 20 minutes from the school and then stand in line for 2 hours because it is a very popular place. Or go to a restaurant that is not so popular where you can be seated as soon as you walk in the door? It is a judgment call. The choice should be voted on by all who are going with you. Time is a crucial element that you need to consider, especially if you are facing a deadline in a writing class or a project that is due soon. Eating out is a treat, something special, and you need to remember how much time you can spare for this treat.

What kind of food do you desire? 想好想吃什么。

Perhaps the biggest question for you to answer is this one. Sure, you are hungry but what are you hungry for? As you put together your group of friends for dinner, each will express what he/she would like to eat for dinner. Sometimes you can find a restaurant that will have the food each person desires, but most of the time this will not work out. Therefore, you must learn to either compromise or convince the others that the kind of food you want to eat is also what they want to eat. We do this a lot when it is a special occasion. For example, if it is someone's birthday, the group will take the birthday boy or girl to the restaurant of their choice, pay for their meal and still give them gifts, a cake and a lot of wonderful memories. If you are sad or hurt about something, your friends will take you where you want to go in order to cheer you up. So time is an important factor. It is relevant for so many different reasons.

Money. 控制好你的钱包。

Since most college students are aware of how much money they can spend for dining out, as a group, they decide beforehand where they will eat. Usually the places are inexpensive or they have specials. An example would be "Happy Hour". Happy Hour is a very popular time of day when a restaurant is open for business and they have various 'specials' that draw people to them. They could advertise that on Fridays college students get 50% off on their drinks. They could advertise that Thursday is Ladies Night

and all ladies get free drinks and appetizers for 2 hours. The specials are developed to pull people in after work or after classes are finished and while the evening is young. College and university students all know about Happy Hour and they can tell you what the specials are at each restaurant near the campus. Eventually you will find yourself either at a few of these restaurants or telling new students about them. Restaurants around a university campus understand that students have limited funds, so they try to make Happy Hour as fun as possible for the students. It's a good situation for the restaurant and a good way for students to relax and let loose.

America, like any other country in the world, has a wide variety of restaurants for you to choose from. The best way, as mentioned earlier, is to decide and vote as a group for the restaurant of the evening. You can always go to other places in the future. If it is your first time going to a particular restaurant, do not worry, there is probably someone else in your group who has never been there either. Just go and enjoy your friends, the atmosphere and the food.

One problem that foreign students face when going to a new restaurant is what to order from the menu. Most foreign students find this to be a daunting task and they get very nervous about it. Later in this section you will find some dialogues that will help you overcome your fear of what to say in a restaurant. Dining out should be a unique experience, something you will remember for a long time. It should never make you nervous or uneasy. You will have your friends with you, so if you see something on the menu and you don't know what it is, ask one of your friends. If they don't know, they will ask the waiter or waitress about it.

So, what kinds of problems will you face in a restaurant and how can you solve the problems? This next subsection will give you some insight.

The Do's and Don'ts in a Restaurant 餐厅行为准则

你知道在国外就餐要注意些什么吗？用餐时会遇到什么问题又该如何解决，在外用餐需要了解哪些餐桌礼仪？下面我们就会提供给大家一份就餐宝典，它简单易学，保证大家读过后能将种种难题一一化解，尽情享受餐厅时光。

Most of the do's and don'ts about restaurants come from common sense. However, there are some cultural issues that you should be aware of. This subsection will look at what happens in a restaurant, what types of problems (if any) you might encounter and how to solve them. Knowing these things will make your time in a foreign restaurant more enjoyable and easier to manage.

1. Reservations. 预定。

If you are going to a nice restaurant with friends, it might be a good idea to call ahead and see if they take reservations. We reserve tables in a restaurant so we do not have to stand and wait in line. If there is a special occasion, such as a birthday, a reservation makes the event easier on everybody. Imagine going to a restaurant for your birthday and no one made a reservation. You get to the restaurant and they tell you that there is a 2-hour wait until you can be seated. Now that does not sound like fun, does it? If you want to make the evening fun and enjoyable, take a moment and call the restaurant and ask if you can make a reservation. If they say yes, they will ask for your name and how many people are in your party. They will also ask you for the date and time. Usually, it is very difficult to set up a reservation on the same day you plan to eat out. So, plan ahead and make a reservation at least 1 week in advance. In cities like New York, popular

restaurants take reservations several months in advance. Extremely popular places will set reservations 1 year in advance. It is only a short phone call, but if you can do so you will not be standing in a long line thinking about how hungry you are.

2.Specials of the Day. 当日特价菜品。

When you are seated, ask your waiter or waitress what the specials of the day are. The specials are usually selected by the chef and prepared only for that day. Specials could run for one day only or for a week. It depends on the chef and the restaurant manager. Specials are not the average food on the menu. That is why they are called specials. The waiter or waitress will tell you what drinks, appetizers, main dishes and desserts are specials. Once you have heard them, you can make your choice of a special or select something from the menu. Most people seem to choose one of the specials, especially if they have become a regular customer of the restaurant. The restaurant uses Specials of the Day to try out new items that they might add to their menu in the future. They also use it during special events. A good example would be Valentine's Day on February 14th. Valentine's Day is a day for lovers. When a couple comes to the restaurant, one special of the day might be a drink that 2 people can share. Another special might be a dessert served with 2 spoons. If a restaurant has Specials of the Day, they will advertise the specials on a sign so that every customer entering the establishment can see them. Even if you see the sign and you have already decided what you would like to order good manners dictates that you should ask about the specials.

Depending on the restaurant and how it is run, there might be times when you are seated and the waiter or waitress will come to your table and tell you what the specials are without having to be asked. It simply depends on the management and how they want their staff to work.

3.Drinks. 饮料。

Usually when you are first seated, the waitperson will ask you if you want a drink. While they are getting your drink, they are also giving you time to look over the menu to choose what you want for dinner. It is all about manners and not pressuring the customer. As a university student, you need to know that every state in the United States has their own laws about alcohol consumption. The legal age in most states is 21. If you are not 21 you cannot be served an alcoholic drink. Always carry your student ID with you so you can show them just how old you are. If you are not sure what you want to drink you can ask the waitperson for suggestions or ask your friends. They will tell you about different drinks they have tried and they usually tell you what is good or bad.

4.Appetizers. 开胃菜。

When you have placed your drink order, the group you are with will begin looking at appetizers in the menu. Appetizers are commonly known as "finger food". Appetizers are small quantities of food that are used to curb your appetite until your main course comes to the table. Most appetizers are eaten by using your fingers or a small fork or spoon. Many people make the mistake of ordering too many appetizers and when their main course finally comes out, they are too full to eat it. So, when it comes to appetizers your group can decide on what to get (and share) while waiting for the main course to be prepared. Obviously, if you are simply waiting for your main dish, you do not have to get an appetizer. It is your choice.

5.Main Dishes. 主食。

When you are ordering the main dishes you wish to eat, it is a good

idea to ask the waitperson what comes with the dish. Sometimes it will have a salad and bread or pasta or even nothing. Knowing what you are actually getting beforehand makes your decision easier to make. So do not be afraid to ask. It is your right as the customer and it is the duty of the waitperson to inform you.

6.Desserts. 甜品。

In the US desserts are always served at the end of the meal. In a restaurant menu, desserts are at the end of the menu. You will notice that the menu is set up as: drinks, appetizers, main dishes, desserts. So after you have finished your main course, the waiter or waitress will come and ask you if you would like dessert. If you say yes, they will hand you the menu. Some restaurants have a separate dessert menu. You can ask about any dessert in the menu and the waitperson will tell you how it is made, what it tastes like, etc. It is part of their job to introduce their products.

7.Asking for the bill or check. 买单。

At the end of the dinner you need to pay the bill. You simply hold up your hand and your waiter or waitress will come to your table. All you have to say is, "Can I have the check, please?" or "Can I have the bill please?" And they will hand it to you. In nicer restaurants, the waitperson will tell you when they hand you the bill that they will take it for you when you are ready. This means that you put your money in a folder where the bill is located and hand it to your waiter or waitress. They will take it to the cashier and get your change for you. If you decide to use a credit card, you place your credit card in the folder and they will process your bill for you. They will return with a sales slip for you to sign and the transaction is complete. However, using a credit card also means you must decide how much you wish to add on to the bill for a gratuity or tip for the waiter or waitress. Again, in nicer restaurants the tip is already included in the bill. It will be added on and you can see it on the sales slip that you need to sign. If you are paying in cash, the rule for tipping is that you take the sales tax listed on the bill and multiply it by 20. This means you are paying the waiter or waitress 20% of the overall bill. This would be a normal amount to pay for their service to you. When using cash, the waiter or waitress will bring you the folder with your change in it. They will thank you for coming to the restaurant and wish you a pleasant evening. When you are handed the folder, you decide how much of a tip to give them and place it in the folder. You have 2 options now: either place the folder on the table and leave or hand it back to your waitperson and thank them for their service.

8.Behavior. 行为检点。

In most American restaurants, people prefer to eat in a comfortable environment with little noise. When people at a particular table start to get loud, it affects the entire restaurant. Management will not tolerate this type of behavior for long and eventually they will ask the patrons to leave. The atmosphere should be quiet and casual, not loud and boisterous. University students can get loud at times, but they should know when to turn down the volume. Always keep in mind that there are other people in the restaurant and they are there to have a pleasant time.

9.Bad service. 糟糕的服务。

One of the things you must remember is that people working in restaurants are human beings. They have good days and bad days just like everyone else. If you encounter a waiter or waitress who is not at his or her best, chances are pretty good that at some point in the evening he or she will apologize to you for what ever problems come up. If you have absolutely no patience in this type of situation, you can ask to speak to the manager.

The manager will come to you and ask you what the problem is and he/she will ask you how you would like it solved. Bad service is not something that happens all the time. The best way to get past it is to keep in mind that the person waiting on your table is human and may be having a bad day.

10.Bad food. 糟糕的食物。

If you order food and it is not to your liking, you can ask your waiter or waitress to take it back to the kitchen. You simply tell them what is wrong and they will try to fix it for you. All they want to do is please you. It is not a big problem. Sometimes food will come out and it is too salty. You tell them and they will make a new dish for you. It might be cold. They will either heat it up or make a new dish for you. It all depends on your taste and your expectations. Never be afraid to complain to your waiter or waitress about the food. They would rather have you complain than have you leave the restaurant without touching your food.

西餐点餐顺序

1. appetizer 开胃品，一般有冷盘和热头盘之分，常见的品种有鱼子酱、鹅肝酱、熏鲑鱼、鸡尾杯。

2. soup 汤，大致可分为清汤、奶油汤、蔬菜汤和冷汤等4类。

3. salad 沙拉，蔬菜类菜肴在西餐中称为沙拉，一般用生菜、番茄、黄瓜、芦笋等制作。

4. Main course (entrée) 主菜，肉、禽类菜肴是主菜。其中最有代表性的是牛肉或牛排。

5. dessert 甜品，它包括所有主菜后的食物，如布丁、冰淇淋、奶酪、水果等等。

6. Coffee/tea service 咖啡或茶

Table setting 西餐餐桌的布置

1. Sherry glass
2. White wine glass
3. Red wine glass
4. Water goblet
5. Seafood fork
6. Soup spoon
7. Dinner knife
8. Dinner fork
9. Salad fork
10. Dessert fork and spoon
11. Butter plate

Vocabulary

cafeteria ['kæfi'tiəriə] n. 自助餐厅

pace [peis] n. 速度,步调,步法

accomplish [ə'kɔmpliʃ] v. 完成

venture ['ventʃə] v. 敢尝试,冒险一试

variety [və'raiəti] n. 多样,种类

guideline ['gaidlain] n. 指引

merely ['miəli] ad. 仅仅,只不过

directions [di'rekʃən, dai'rekʃən] n. 方向

suitable ['sju:təbl] a. 合适的,适宜的

rely [ri'lai] v. 信赖,倚赖

public transportation 公共交通

budget ['bʌdʒit] n. 预算

mention ['menʃən] vt. 说起，提到

reasonable ['ri:znəbl] a. 合理的，有道理的，适度

obtain [əb'tein] vt. 获得，得到

focus ['fəukəs] n. 焦点，焦距

conservative [kən'sə:vətiv] a. 保守的

frugal ['fru:gəl] a. 节俭的

thrifty ['θrifti] a. 节俭的，节约的

advantage [əd'vɑ:ntidʒ] n. 优势，有利条件

convince [kən'vins] v. 说服，使...相信

clothes [kləuðz] n. 衣服

schedule ['skedʒjul] n. 时间表，一览表，计划

maintain [men'tein] v. 维持，维修，保养，坚持

judgment ['dʒʌdʒmənt] n. 裁判，宣告，判决书

crucial ['kru:ʃiəl, 'kru:ʃl] a. 关键的，决定性的

consider [kən'sidə] v. 考虑，思考，认为

especially [is'peʃəli] ad. 特别，尤其

deadline ['dedlain] n. 最后期限

project ['prɔdʒekt] n. 工程，项目

treat [tri:t] n. 宴飨，款待

special ['speʃəl] a. 特别的，专门的

express [iks'pres] v. 表达，表示

compromise ['kɔmprəmaiz] v. 妥协，让步

occasion [ə'keiʒən] n. 场合，机会，理由

memory ['meməri] n. 记忆

cheer [tʃiə] v. 加油，鼓舞，快活起来

factor ['fæktə] n. 因素，因子
relevant ['relivənt] a. 相关的，切题的
beforehand [bi'fɔ:hænd] ad. 预先，事先
inexpensive [iniks'pensiv] a. 不贵的
Happy Hour 快乐时间，减价供应饮料等的时间
Various ['vɛəriəs] a. 各种各样的
draw [drɔ:] v. 拉，拖，挨近
advertise ['ædvətaiz] v. 登广告
appetizer ['æpə,taizər] n. 开胃的食物
develop [di'veləp] v. 开发
pull [pul] vt. 拉
young [jʌŋ] a. 年轻的，新兴的，有朝气的
eventually [i'ventjuəli] ad. 终于，最后
limited funds 有限的资金
situation [sitju'eiʃən] n. 位置，形势，局面
let loose 放松
atmosphere ['ætməsfiə] n. 大气，气氛
menu ['menju:] n. 菜单
daunting [dɔntiŋ] a. 令人生畏的
nervous ['nə:vəs] a. 紧张的
overcome [əuvə'kʌm] v. 战胜，克服
unique [ju:'ni:k] a. 独一无二的，独特的，稀罕的
uneasy [ʌn'i:zi] a. 不自在的，心神不安的
waiter ['weitə] n. 侍者，服务员
waitress ['weitris] n. 女侍者，女服务员
subsection ['sʌb'sekʃən] n. 小部份，小单位，细分
common sense 常识（尤指判断力）

cultural ['kʌltʃərəl] n. 文化的，文化上的

encounter [in'kauntə] v. 遇到，偶然碰到，遭遇

reservation [rezə'veiʃən] n. 预定

reserve [ri'zə:v] v. 保留，预订

imagine [i'mædʒin] v. 想像，幻想，猜测

moment ['məumənt] n. 片刻，瞬间

Special ['speʃəl] n. 专辑，专车，特色菜

Chef [ʃef] n. 厨师

average ['ævəridʒ] a. 一般的，通常的，平均的

dessert [di'zə:t] n. 甜食

Valentine's Day 情人节

Spoon [spu:n] n. 匙

Establishment [is'tæbliʃmənt] n. 确立，制定，设施

dictate [dik'teit] v. 命令，指挥，指令

staff [stɑ:f] n. 全体人员，同事

waitperson [' weitpə:sn] n. (餐厅、旅馆的)服务员

manners ['mænəz] n. 礼貌，规范，风度

pressure ['preʃə(r)] v. 催促

customer ['kʌstəmə] n. 顾客

alcohol ['ælkəhɔl] n. 酒精

consumption [kən'sʌmpʃən] n. 消费

legal ['li:gəl] a. 法律的，合法的，法定的

alcoholic [ælkə'hɔ:lik] a. 酒精性的

finger food 零食

quantity ['kwɔntiti] n. 量，数量，大量

curb [kə:b] v. 抑制，束缚

appetite ['æpitait] n. 爱好，嗜好，食欲，胃口，欲望

mistake [mis'teik] n. 错误, 误会
prepare [pri'pεə] v. 准备, 预备
obviously ['ɔbviəsli] ad. 显然地
salad ['sæləd] n. 色拉
bread [bred] n. 面包
pasta ['pɑ:stə] n. 生面团, 意大利通心粉
duty ['dju:ti] n. 责任, 职责
inform [in'fɔ:m] v. 告诉, 通知
separate ['sepəreit] a. 分开的, 各自的, 单独的
product ['prɔdəkt] n. 产品, 成果
bill [bil] n. 帐单,, 票据
check [tʃek] 发票, 收据
folder ['fəuldə] n. 文件夹, 纸夹
locate [ləu'keit] v. 设于, 位于
cashier [kə'ʃiə] n. 出纳员, 收银员
change [tʃeindʒ] n. 变化, 零钱
credit card 信用卡
process [prə'ses] v. 加工, 处理
sales slip 销售(货)单, 销售(货)发票
transaction [træn'zækʃən] n. 交易, 处理, 办理
complete [kəm'pli:t] a. 彻底的, 完整的, 已完成的
gratuity [grə'tju(:)iti] n. 小费, 赏钱
tip [tip] n. 小费 v. 给小费
sales tax 销售税
multiply ['mʌltiplai] v. 乘, 繁殖, 增加
overall ['əuvərɔ:l] a. 全部的, 全体的
pleasant ['plezənt] a. 令人愉快的, 舒适的

option ['ɔpʃən] n. 选择
behavior [bi'heiviə] n. 行为，举止
prefer [pri'fə:] v. 较喜欢，宁可
environment [in'vaiərənmənt] n. 环境
noise [nɔiz] n. 声音，响声，喧哗声，噪声
loud [laud] a. 大声的
affect [ə'fekt] v. 影响，作用
tolerate ['tɔləreit] v. 容忍，忍受，容许
patron ['peitrən, 'pæ-] n. 老顾客，赞助人
quiet ['kwaiət] a. 安静的，静止的，宁静的
casual ['kæʒjuəl] a. 随便的，非正式的
boisterous ['bɔistərəs] a. 喧闹的，吵闹的
turn down the volume 调低音量
apologize [ə'pɔlədʒaiz] v. 道歉
patience ['peiʃəns] n. 耐心
liking ['laikiŋ] n. 爱好，嗜好
kitchen ['kitʃin] n. 厨房
fix [fiks] v. 修理
salty ['sɔ:lti] a. 咸的
taste [teist] n. 味道，口味
expectation [ekspek'teiʃən] n. 期待，期望
afraid [ə'freid] a. 害怕的，担心的
complain [kəm'plein] v. 抱怨，控诉
rather ['rɑ:ðə] ad. 宁可，宁愿
touch [tʌtʃ] v. 接触，触及

Conversation Questions

1. Do you care what a restaurant looks like, or is the food the only thing you care about?
2. What do you think about people smoking in a restaurant when you are trying to eat?
3. How often do you eat out?
4. Where do you usually go when you eat out?
5. How much do you usually pay when you eat out?
6. Who do you usually go with when you eat out?
7. Would you send a dish back if it did not taste good or if you received the wrong food?
8. Do you ever leave a tip at a restaurant?
9. What's the worst experience you ever had at a restaurant?
10. Do you like to try new restaurants, or do you prefer to go to those you have already been to? Why?

Discussion Questions

1. What would be a big difference between western restaurants and Chinese restaurants?
2. If you were to travel to another country, would you try other kinds of food or would you go to a Chinese restaurant? Why?
3. In the US we say that if you eat Chinese food for dinner, 30 minutes later you will be hungry again. What does that mean to you?

4.Would you be afraid to try western food?

5.Discuss with your partner the cultural differences between China and the West regarding food.

6.Will the Chinese people ever accept western food into their daily diet?

7.If you eat western food, what is your favorite?

8.Chinese food is very popular in America. What do you think of it?

9.Have you ever encountered disruptive behavior while in a restaurant? How did you handle it?

10.Have you ever complained to the manager about service or food? What happened and how was the problem resolved?

Practice Dialogues

Throughout this book you will have a variety of dialogues that you can use to practice speaking and asking questions. Each section of the book will have 3 dialogues for your use.

Dialogue # 1 – Student and the RA

S: Hi. Can I ask you a few questions?

RA: Sure. What do you want to know?

S: Well, a few of us are going out to eat next week because it is my birthday.

RA: Well, happy birthday!

S: Thanks so much. I have not been to a restaurant off campus and I want to know about a few that might be near the school.

RA: Well, there are many restaurants near the campus. What kind of

food do you want to try?

S: I'm not sure. There are 2 of us from China and 1 from Sweden. The others are from America. About 6 people will go to dinner and they all have different tastes for food.

RA: Let me see. Come to my office, I have some things that might make it easier for you.

S: Okay.

RA: Here are the menus for some places near the campus. You can actually walk to any of them. It would take you about 10 minutes to get there.

S: Great. Can I share these with the other students?

RA: Sure. But when you are finished, make sure you bring them back to me. I use them to plan a party at the end of the semester before summer starts.

S: Oh that sounds like fun.

RA: It is a lot of fun, but a lot of work too. I think you will enjoy it when it comes around.

S: Me? Oh I am sure I will enjoy it. Thanks for the menus. I will bring them back soon.

RA: Okay. If your birthday party is next week, you might think about calling and making a reservation. The restaurants near the campus are always popular. It would be much convenient for your group if you have a reservation set up.

S: Thanks for the suggestion. I will call once we decide where we are going.

RA: Okay. See you later then.

S: Right and thanks again for your help.

RA: You're welcome.

Dialogue #2 – Student /Restaurant Phone Call

R: Michael's Restaurant, can I help you?

S: Yes, I would like to make a reservation, please?

R: Okay, let me get some information from you.

S: Okay.

R: what is your last name?

S: My last name is _____.

R: Okay. And how many people are in your party?

S: 6 people.

R: Good. Now what day would you like to make the reservation for?

S: I would like it for a week from this coming Friday.

R: So, next week on Friday?

S: Yes.

R: And what time would you like to come to the restaurant?

S: We would like to set the reservation for 7pm.

R: Okay. Do you want to sit inside or outside?

S: Gee, I didn't know you had seating outside. Let me think for a second.

R: Take your time, no rush.

S: Thank you. Hmmm, I think we will sit inside.

R: Very good. So let me read back your reservation to you.

S: Okay.

R: That is a reservation for _____, a party of 6 for next Friday at 7pm inside the restaurant. Correct?

S: Yes, that's right.

R: Great. Is there anything else I can help you with?

S: I'm not sure. I am planning the party because it is my birthday and I want it to be special since this is my first time in America.

R: Oh well, everything will be taken care of next Friday. Do not worry, it's your birthday and it should be a special occasion.

S: Thank you for your help. We will see you next week.

R: Okay. Have a good weekend, see you next week.

Dialogue #3 – At the Restaurant

Hostess (H): Good evening and welcome to Michael's. Do you have a reservation?

S: Yes, the reservation is under the name_____.

H: Oh yes, a party of 6?

S: Yes, that's right.

H: Follow me please.

S: Thank you.

H: Here's your table. Please have a seat. Your waiter will be over soon.

S: Thank you.

W: Hello, my name is David. I will be your waiter this evening.

S: Hi David.

W: Would you like any drinks from the bar?

S: Yes, we would like a large pitcher of beer, please.

W: Very good. While I am getting your drinks, please look through the menu. If you look over there on the wall you can see the specials we have for this evening. I will answer any questions you have when I return with your drinks.

S: Okay, thanks.

W: Now, what would you like to order?

S: I think we want to order 3 of your specials: the extra large pizza, the cheese bread and the pasta salad.

W: Sounds good. Is there anything else you want to order?

S: No, not right now.

W: Very well, I will put your order in.

S: Thank you David.

W: My pleasure.

W: Here is your extra large pizza, bread and pasta salad. Enjoy your meal.

S: Thanks.

W: Would anyone care for dessert or coffee?

S: I'm not sure. Give us a moment to talk about it.

W: No problem. Just wave and I will come to you.

S: David we would like some tea please.

W: Green tea? Red tea? Black tea?

S: Green tea would be nice.

W: I will bring 2 pots of tea for the table.

S: Great. Thank you!

W: According to the hostess and manager, it is your birthday today. So the staff would like to give you this birthday cake and we all wish you a very happy birthday.

S: Wow! Thank you so much! It looks so good. Can I give you a piece of the cake David?

W: Sure, if you wish. I can eat it later when I am on break.

S: Well here. Take this piece and enjoy it.

W: Thank you very much.

S: Thank you David. This has turned out to be a wonderful birthday.

Chapter 4
Contacts and facing problems/solving problems

紧急联系电话及面对问题／解决问题

Guided Reading

在学校安顿下来后,你需要告知学校你的联系人的联系方式,以防万一需要联系你的家人或朋友。在学校,你会碰到各种各样的问题,比如与同学相处不融洽、生病、丢失财物、学习跟不上等,这时候你该怎么办?你该找谁来帮助你呢?这一章将告诉你碰到以上情形该如何处理。

After you arrive at your school and have settled in, you need to write a list of people you need to keep in contact with. Of course at the top of the list would be your parents. You would also include any friends that you have regular correspondence with. In addition to your parents and friends, you should include a few of the people in your dormitory. The reason for developing this list is quite simple: if something happens to you, people will know who to contact on your behalf. In most universities, when a new student arrives at the dormitory, the RA will let them fill out a piece of paper listing contacts and contact numbers. If you happen to get a part time job either on campus or off campus, it would be a good idea to add them to your list as well. If you become ill, one of your friends can call your workplace for you. Keep your list either in your desk drawer or tape it on the wall near your desk so that you can see it and it can be seen by others.

Every university student inevitably faces some problems during the course of their education. What types of problems will you face when you are in a new school? Well, listed below are common problems you might face and suggestions on how to handle them. The problems will vary, but in most cases the solutions are similar.

Problem	Solution
Loud noise	Ask them to stop or call your RA.
Cheating on an exam	Speak to the teacher privately.
Lost a book	Post a note in the dormitory.
Lost keys	Post a note in the dormitory or see RA.
Stolen property	Speak to the RA privately.
Illness	Go to the clinic on campus first.
Missing class	Call the teacher if possible.
Missing work	Call the employer.

遗失物品启示 范文

Lost Note

10/22/2011

　　Lost gold Canon PowerShot SD960 IS on way from A Street to Tercero living area. Around 10p.m. on Saturday night, biked on Hutchinson Drive, cut through Everson, past Roessler, and onto Bainer Hall Dr. Please contact me at bh1548@gmail.com if you found it! Or phone me:12345678 (: Thanks in advance!

写遗失物品启示时一定要注意以下几大要素：

时间

地点

物品

联系方式

主要留学目的地报警求救号码表

国家	紧急求救	警察	火警	救护车	交通事故	查号台
新加坡	999	999	995	999		
马来西亚	112	999	995	999		103
印度		100	101	102	103	
英国	999/112					
法国	112	17		15		
美国	911					
德国			110	112	112	
日本			110	119		
芬兰	112		10022			
爱尔兰	999/112					
意大利			113	115	118	
瑞士			117		118	
巴西			190	193	192	
澳大利亚	000					
加拿大	911					

There will be many problems that you might face while in school. The best source for solving these problem is your RA. He/she has been trained to handle various problems that students have while in the dormitory. So if you are ever in doubt, talk to your RA first. He/she will help you as much as they possibly can. If they can't help you directly, they will point you in the right direction to someone who can help you. The key is not to worry too much.

Let's return to contacts for a few minutes. If you are in an office in the university or even out in public and you are speaking to someone, make sure you get their name. Write it down and keep it or put it in your telephone. That person will become a contact person the next time you need to visit that office. They might not remember you, but calling and asking for that person will make your next visit to the office easier. Besides, you might be making a new friend too.

If you are having difficulties with your classes, the best way to solve them is to speak to your teachers. All university teachers have office hours and they will tell you when their office hours are at the beginning of the semester. During the first week of classes your teacher will tell you his/her office hours. Write the hours down and keep them handy in case you need to speak to your teacher. Some teachers prefer it if you make an appointment to see them. They will give you their office phone number, so make sure you keep it. University teachers will help you if you ask them to help you. They do not give second chances like teachers in China do. However, if you are ill or have a valid reason for missing a class or not finishing a paper on time, and you can explain this situation to your teacher, he/she might allow you more time to complete the assignment or make up the class. They can be reasoned with, but never expect them to give you a second chance.

If you are not happy with your grade, you must speak with your teacher about it. He/she is the only person who can help you. If you do not like the class you are in, you can drop the class within the first few weeks of classes. Some schools will allow add/drop classes during the first two weeks. Check with your admissions office to find out for sure.

Perhaps the biggest problem facing students from foreign countries is being homesick. This is understandable and there is very little that can be done to solve it. However, knowing that you will go through a period of adjustment when you reach the other country will make the process go smoother. The regular amount of time needed to adjust to a new environment is 6 months. During that time you will experience a variety of feelings. Firstly, you will feel excited about being in a new place. Within a few weeks the newness will wear off as your daily routine sets in. The next step is merely adjusting to your surroundings; this takes about 3-4 weeks to complete. There is a period of time where you will feel like you do not fit in and want to return to your home country. This is a natural reaction to your surroundings and it will last about 4 weeks. You will also look at things in a different manner. You will compare what you see and experience in the foreign country to what things are like back in China. Finally, you will begin to see your school and friends as your second family and the idea of being homesick will quickly fade, It is a very natural process and we all go through it when we relocate in another country. If you need a little bit of 'home' to keep you happy, try to go out to a Chinese restaurant or to Chinatown for the evening. Take some friends along and explore the town, eat some good food and remind yourself why you came to the US in the first place: to get an education.

One bit of information that you should be keenly aware of is speaking up for yourself when necessary. Chinese students are often seen as quiet and reserved. They prefer to sit outside the circle and observe what is going on instead of being part of the circle. This will be your biggest problem to overcome during the university life. You are graded on what you contribute to the classroom discussion. You are given points for participating in class. You need to figure out how to make yourself heard while in the classroom. It will not help you to meet with the teacher after class to discuss what you have said in class. So, how can you make yourself stand out in the classroom? Use some of these suggestions:

Be prepared ahead of time. Make sure you have completed the readings, writings, or drawings that the teacher has assigned before coming to class.

Location, location, location is a key factor. Place yourself so that the teacher can see you. When you wish to speak, raise your hand up in the air and wait for the teacher to call on you. If you are in a circle, raise your hand and look directly at the teacher. In most foreign countries the teacher doesn't require a student to raise his/her hand. However, it is still a good way to get the teachers' attention.

Anticipate any questions that the teacher may ask. If you are prepared for the class, you can also prepare a list of questions that may be discussed in class. If the teacher asks for questions, be ready to ask one or two questions . The more you participate, the better your grade will be and the more your teacher will appreciate your being in the classroom.

Clarification of an idea or statement is an easy way to get a conversation going. If you have read through your assignment and found something that you do not understand, mark it and bring it to class. You

can ask about it in class and the teacher and students will discuss what it means and try to explain it to you. However, try not to do this too many times, the more you do it eventually someone will ask if you actually read the material to begin with or are you simply asking questions just to waste time. Clarification, while it is a good way to generate a conversation, should be used as a last resort for class participation.

Sit in the front of the classroom in the first row of desks so that the teacher notices you. If you sit in the back you will go unnoticed and you will be forgotten. Sitting in the front tells the teacher that you are a student who wishes to learn. Sitting in the back tells the teacher you really don't care about school and have no idea why you are in the class.

Many students come from China to the US every year. They come for primarily the same reason: to get an education. What they end up getting is much more than just an education. They get a dose of reality. The students find what is good and bad about both China and the US. If they are open-minded they will be able to put those differences into perspective. They will be able to understand the differences and actually appreciate them. Every new student will judge what is going on around him/her. The activity will be given a personal value and either accepted or discarded by the student. The best thing you can do when coming to the US is to keep an open mind. Americans come in all shapes and sizes. Some are nice, some are mean, but your common sense will tell you how to handle each person. Be yourself, be polite and everything will work out fine for you.

How to make an appointment with a professor

怎样跟老师约定会面时间

A: Professor, could I make an appointment with you?

B: I am free tomorrow afternoon between two and four, do you have a particular time in mind?

A: Two o'clock would be the best time.

B: Fine, do you know where my office is?

A: No, I'm not sure.

B: Remember, it is in the E building on the third floor.

A: I see.

B: Don't worry, it will work out fine once you get there. I'll see you then.

A: I'll see you then.

B: Looking forward to meeting with you!

A: Excuse me, Professor, is there a time when I could meet with you?

B: I could meet with you tomorrow anywhere from two until four; what time works out best?

A: I would like to come at three o'clock.

B: I am glad that works out, can you find my office?

A: Yes, I do.

B: Just follow the walkway to the outside and climb the stairs to the third floor.

A: I got it.

B: If you do get lost, just ask someone in the building to point the way.

A: Thank you, I'll be there.

B: If you need to cancel your appointment, please give me a call.

A: Professor, do you have a few moments when I could meet with you?

B: I schedule my appointments from two to four on Saturday, what works best for you?

A: Three would be a good time.

B: Great, do you need directions to my office?

A: I'm not sure.

B: Well, just make sure to go through the double doors, and I'll be on the right.

A: OK, I'll find it.

B: It's very easy to find.

A: See you then.

B: I will enjoy seeing you, have a good week!

Vocabulary

correspondence [ˌkɔːrə'spɔndəns] n. 类似；联系；相当
behalf [bə'hæf] n. 代表
inevitably [ˌi'nevətəbliː] adj. 必然发生的；不可避免的
vary ['veriː] v. 变化；有不同；呈差异
solution [sə'luːʃən] n. 解决方法，解决方案
privately ['praivətliː] adv. 私下地；以私人方式（或身份）
clinic ['klinik] n. （尤指专科）诊所；门诊部
doubt ['daut] v. 疑惑，怀疑

appointment [ə'pɔintmənt] n. 约会，约定

valid ['vælid] adj. 令人信服的，确凿的

homesick ['həum,sik] adj. 想家的，思乡的

understandable [,əndə:'stændəbəl] adj. 可理解的；可了解的

adjustment [ə'dʒəstmənt] v. 调整，整理

process ['prɔ,ses] n. 步骤，程序；方法

smoother ['smu:ðə:] adj. 更光滑的

newness ['nu:nəs] n. 新奇，新鲜感

natural ['nætʃərəl] adj. 自然的，非人为的

reaction [ri:'ækʃən] v. 反应

fade ['feid] v. 渐弱；逐渐消失

relocate [ri:'ləukeit] v. 迁移

keenly ['ki:nli:] adj. 热心的，热切的

reserved [rə'zə:vd] adj. 预定的，保留的，拘谨的

contribute [kən'tribju:t] v. 捐助，捐献；贡献

stand out 突出；显眼

anticipate [æn'tisə,peit] v. 期望；预料

clarification [,klerəfi'keiʃən] v. 澄清，清洁；净化

eventually [i'ventjuəli:] adv. 最终；终于

generate ['dʒenəreit] v. 引发（某种情感）；造成（某种情况）；使……发生

reasoned with 推理

unnoticed [,ʌn'nəutist] adj. 未被觉察到的，未被注意到的；不受人注意的，被忽视的；没人理睬的

forgotten [fə'gɔtn] v. 忘记（forget 的过去分词）

dose [dəus] n. 剂量，药量；一服，一剂

reality [ri'æliti] n. 现实，现实性；真实情况

judge [dʒʌdʒ] vt.& vi. 审判，评判；断定

polite[pə'lait] adj. 有礼貌的；有教养的

perspective [pə'spektiv] n. 观点，看法

discarded [dis'kɑ:did] v. 丢弃，抛弃 (discard 的过去式和过去分词)；不再使用

accepted [ək'septid] adj. 公认的；可以接受的 v. 接受 (accept 的过去式及过去分词)

Conversation Questions

1. Do you like living with others or alone? Why?

2. Do you help others or let them do things by themselves?

3. What was the worst argument you have ever had?

4. If you are a quiet person, how do you make yourself noticed?

5. Is it better to be quiet or talkative? Why?

6. Do you have self-confidence?

7. Are you independent or do you rely on others for help? Why?

8. Are you a leader or a follower? Why?

9. Have you ever lost an argument?

10. Do you like to fight with others? Why?

Discussion Questions

1. Do you have a hard time when you express yourself with foreigners?

2. When you travel do you need to call your parents?

3. What is the best way to reach your parents?

4. What kind of student are you: quiet/reserved or open/active?

5. Do you ever get into arguments with your parents of friends?

6. How do you deal with conflicts?

7. Are you easy to live with? Why?

8. When you came to college were you homesick? Why?

9. What can you do to keep from being homesick?

10. Tell me about a problem you had with your roommates?

Practice Dialogues

Throughout this book you will have a variety of dialogues that you can use to practice speaking and asking questions. Each section of the book will have 3 dialogues for your use.

Dialogue # 1 – Student and the RA

S: Hi, can I talk to you for a minute?

RA: Sure, come in.

S: Thanks. I need to change a class but I don't know how. Can you help me?

RA: No problem. What class are you changing?

S: I need to change my English class from 8a.m. to 10a.m. class.

RA: Is there a reason why you want to change classes?

S: Not really, except all my classes begin at 10a.m. except the English one.

RA: Oh, so you want to sleep in on that day instead of having to get up early for the class?

S: I guess so.

RA: Have 2 weeks passed since classes began?

S: No, we have a few more days left in this week. Why?

RA: The policy for changing classes is that you can do so within the first 2 weeks of classes. You don't have to give a reason for the change, you simply have to fill out the add/drop form in the registrar's office.

S: Oh, so I have to go to the Registrar's Office, fill out the add/drop form and hand it in?

RA: Yep. Make sure you take along your student ID so they can change it quickly for you.

S: Great! Thanks for your help.

RA: Oh, one other thing. When you change classes, make sure who the new teacher is. He/she might have a different book for you to use. That would mean a trip over to the bookstore to buy another book.

S: Oh, not a problem. It's the same teacher. She said it would be no problem for me to change.

RA: well then, you are all set to go.

S: thanks again for your help. I appreciate it.

RA: Any time. See you later.

S: Bye.

Dialogue #2 – Student at Registrar's Office

Clerk: Next?

S: Hi. I want to change classes.

Clerk: Have you filled out the add/drop slip?

S: Yes, I have.

Clerk: Okay, everything looks good. Can I see your ID card?

S: Sure, here you are.

Clerk: Okay, let me check everything in the computer. Alright, you have been changed to 10a.m. English class. Same teacher, same classroom.

S: Thank you.

Clerk: No problem. Just remember, if you want to change classes do it before the 2 week deadline.

S: What happens if I wait until after the 2 weeks is up?

Clerk: Well, there is a lot of paperwork involved. You have to speak to the professors and get permission from them. We have to call them and verify everything. It takes a while to process everything. The worst part is that the professors don't have to let you in their class. They begin classes and cover all the rules in the first few days. Then they hand out assignments. For a student to come in to the class later than 2 weeks means that student is behind at the start. So professors have to make the decision to let a student in or not.

S: I understand.

Clerk: If you want to change classes, make sure you are doing it for the right reasons.

S: Got it. Thanks for the help and the advice.

Clerk: Not at all. Have a great semester.

Dialogue #3 – Student and Professor

P: So, I understand you wish to drop my morning class and move to my 10a.m. class?

S: Yes, ma'am.

P: Why do you want to change classes?

S: Well, your class is the only one on my schedule for 8a.m..

P: Oh, so you want to sleep in instead of getting up and coming to my class?

S: Yes and no.

P: What do you mean, yes and no?

S: Yes, I want to get more sleep, but I prefer to be more organized. My schedule is all set up with 10a.m. classes except yours. I think it would be better if I had all 10a.m. classes.

P: or 8a.m. classes.

S: Well, yes.

P: So, are you always like this? This predictable? This calculated?

S: I guess I am. Why?

P: You are coming from another country to the US. You are also in a university and things are not always predictable or calculated here. Want some advice?

S: Yes, please.

P: Try to be less organized, especially when it comes to your schedule.

S: So you are saying I should be more flexible?

P: Right. When you study for your classes, you can be as organized as you wish. But setting up a schedule should not be rigid or set in stone. University life is not like school back in your country. We do not require students to be up at a certain hour or in bed at a certain hour. We put that responsibility on you. So keep your schedule loose. Allow things to happen during the day and eventually you will find that your days are filled with different happenings.

S: I see what you mean. However, I do have one question for you.

P: Okay, what is your question?

S: Can I loosen up my schedule next semester and just move from your 8a.m. class to your 10a.m. class for now?

P: Of course. Only if you promise to change your schedule up next semester.

S: I promise.

P: Okay, now you need to head to the Registrar's Office to fill out the add/drop form for class changes.

S: Thank you for your time.

P: Not at all. My office hours are set for a reason.

S: Good bye. See you in class tomorrow.

P: I certainly hope so.

Chapter 5
American Holidays

美国的节假日

Guided Reading

每个国家都有自己的传统节假日,美国也有不少,让咱们来具体了解一下美国的传统节假日吧。

When you are in the US, you will find out about the different holidays that are celebrated each year. This section looks at the holidays and gives you some information about each one. Many of the holidays listed are 'federal' holidays. This means that the government shuts down for the day, banks, post offices and other government buildings are also closed. Most universities have no scheduled classes on these days too. As the holidays approach, you will know about them just by watching and talking to the people around you. By the way, at the beginning of the school year, the Registrar's Office will publish the holiday schedule for the academic year. Students use this publication to plan vacations, trips back home, etc. Make sure you get a copy and put it on your wall so you can remember when classes are not scheduled. The publication will also inform you about exams and when they are held. So here is the list and what special activities are planned for each.

New Year's Day 新年

New Year's Day is January 1st. The celebration of this holiday begins the night before, when Americans gather to wish each other a happy and prosperous coming year. Many Americans make New Year's resolutions. A New Year's resolution is a promise to oneself. The most popular promise Americans make to themselves is to lose weight. The second most popular resolution is to stop smoking. Unfortunately, most Americans do not keep their resolutions and they tend to last for a few weeks at best. However, some people are more motivated and they complete their promises. The resolutions are for the entire calendar year.

Birthday of Martin Luther King, Jr. 马丁·路德·金诞辰纪念日

Martin Luther King, Jr. Day is celebrated on the third Monday in January. The Reverend Martin Luther King, Jr. was an African-American clergyman who is recognized for his tireless efforts to win civil rights for all people through non-violent means. Usually there are parades and conventions during this day. The main focus of this day is to continue Dr. King's message of equality for all people. Leading up to this holiday, public schools will spend class time talking about Dr. King and how he inspired so many people. All schools, banks and other government buildings are closed. This is what Americans called a long weekend: Saturday, Sunday and Monday.

Washington's Birthday 乔治·华盛顿诞辰纪念日

Washington's Birthday is observed the third Monday of February in honor of George Washington, the first President of the United States. This date is commonly called Presidents' Day and many groups honor the legacy of past presidents on this date. Small towns and cities have a parade on this day. Almost every major retail store in the US will have some sort of President's Day Sale.

Memorial Day （美国）阵亡将士纪念日

Memorial Day is observed the last Monday of May. It originally honored the people killed in the American Civil War, but has become a day on which the American dead of all wars are remembered. On Memorial Day the

President visits the National Cemetery in Washington, DC and places a wreath at the Tomb of the Unknown Soldier. The tomb is symbolic because it represents all the soldiers who have died in wars protecting their country. Families throughout America visit the graves of family members who were lost in the war. They place small flags by the gravesite, leave flowers and recall the people who have departed. Memorial Day also marks the first week of summer. People spend time either by traveling, being outdoors or shopping. At the university classes will not be scheduled. Most of your roommates will be talking about having a picnic or playing some sports. Memorial Day is another "long" weekend. Your university will have some events planned for the weekend.

Independence Day 美国独立纪念日

Independence Day is July 4th. This holiday honors the nation's birthday - the adoption of the Declaration of Independence on July 4th, 1776. It is a day of picnics and patriotic parades, a night of concerts, and fireworks. The 4th of July is one of the biggest holidays in America. Almost every city will have a fireworks display as soon as the sun sets. Lots of people visit friends, spend time outside or go shopping. Retail stores launch massive sales for this holiday knowing that people will not be sitting at home. If you are with friends during the summer, you will be able to see the fireworks. Unfortunately the fireworks only last one day not several weeks during Spring Festival like in China.

Labor Day 劳动节

Labor Day is the first Monday of September. This holiday honors the nation's working people, typically with parades. For most Americans' it marks the end of the summer vacation season and the start of the school year. Labor Day is now considered as the 'back-to-school' shopping day. All major retail stores will have sales for students going back to school. This is also the time when new students are arriving and settling in at the university. Classes usually begin the next day. On the university campus, Labor Day is filled with excitement. Students are returning and seeing old friends that they haven't seen since the beginning of summer. Most universities will have events planned for Labor Day weekend. This holiday is another 'long' weekend.

Columbus Day 哥伦布纪念日

Columbus Day is celebrated on the second Monday in October. The day commemorates October 12, 1492, when Italian navigator Christopher Columbus landed in the New World. The holiday was first proclaimed in 1937 by President Franklin D. Roosevelt. While Columbus Day is considered a holiday, the only event that happens is retailers having large sales events. Elementary schools will promote the holiday by having students study Christopher Columbus in class and drawing pictures about his voyage.

Veterans Day 退伍军人节

Veterans Day is celebrated on November 11th. This holiday was originally called Armistice Day and established to honor Americans who had served in World War I. It now honors veterans of all wars in which the U.S. has fought. Veterans' organizations hold parades, and the president places a wreath on the Tomb of the Unknown Soldier at Arlington National Cemetery in Virginia.

Thanksgiving Day 感恩节

Thanksgiving Day is celebrated on the fourth Thursday in November. In the fall of 1621, the Pilgrims held a three-day feast to celebrate a bountiful harvest. Many regard this event as the nation's first Thanksgiving. The Thanksgiving feast became a national tradition and almost always includes some of the foods served at the first feast: roast turkey, cranberry sauce, potatoes, and pumpkin pie. Inevitably as a university student you will be invited to someone's house for Thanksgiving. This tradition marks the beginning of the "Holiday Season". Families gather together to spend time catching up on what has been happening over the year. They also plan what will happen at Christmas. The day after Thanksgiving Day is called "Black Friday." This is the first day of the Christmas season. Most of the retail stores will open just after midnight and sell as much as they can possibly sell. It is referred to as black Friday because the retail stores make a lot of money, and they are 'in the black'.

感恩节 Thanksgiving Day：11 月的第四个星期四是感恩节。感恩节是美国人民独创的一个古老节日，也是美国人合家欢聚的节日，因此美国人提起感恩节总是备感亲切。感恩节是美国国定假日中最地道、最美国式的节日，它和早期美国历史最为密切相关。1620 年，一些朝拜者乘坐"五月花"号船去美洲寻求宗教自由。他们在海上颠簸了两个月

之后，终于在酷寒的十一月里，在现在的马萨诸塞州的普利茅斯登陆。

在第一个冬天，半数以上的移民都死于饥饿和传染病，活下来的人们在第一个春季即1621年开始播种。整个夏天他们都热切地盼望着丰收的到来，他们深知自己的生存以及殖民地的存在都将取决于即将到来的收成。最后，庄稼获得了意外的丰收，为了感谢上帝赐予的丰收，举行了3天的狂欢活动。从此，这一习俗就沿续下来，并逐渐风行各地。1863年，美国总统林肯宣布每年十一月的第四个星期四为感恩节。感恩节庆祝活动便定在这一天，直到如今。届时，家家团聚、举国同庆，其盛大、热烈的情形，不亚于中国人过春节。

感恩节庆祝模式许多年来从未改变。丰盛的家宴早在几个月之前就开始着手准备。人们在餐桌上可以吃到苹果、桔子、栗子、胡桃和葡萄，还有葡萄干布丁、碎肉馅饼、各种其他食物以及红莓苔汁和鲜果汁，其中最妙和最吸引人的大菜是烤火鸡和南瓜馅饼，这些菜一直是感恩节中最富于传统和最受人喜爱的食品。

Christmas Day 圣诞节

Christmas Day is celebrated on December 25th. Christmas is a Christian holiday marking the birth of the Christ Child. Decorating houses and yards with lights, putting up Christmas trees, giving gifts, and sending greeting cards have become holiday traditions even for many non-Christian Americans. Today, Christmas is more commercial than it is religious. It is all about giving gifts, receiving gifts, seeing old friends or family members and spending time with loved ones. Many people will attend midnight services on Christmas Eve, the night before Christmas Day, to welcome in the birth of the Christ Child. The day after Christmas Day is called the 'Red' day. This is when people start returning gifts to the stores to either get their money back or exchange them for something else. The retail stores lose a lot of money on this day which means they are 'in the red'.

圣诞节 Christmas：

"圣诞节"这个名称是"基督弥撒"的缩写。弥撒是教会的一种礼拜仪式。人们把圣诞节当作耶稣的诞辰来庆祝，因而又名耶诞节。

12月25日这一天，不论是否礼拜天，世界所有的基督教会都举行特别的礼拜仪式。但是有很多圣诞节的欢庆活动和宗教并无半点关联。交换礼物，寄圣诞卡，这都使圣诞节成为一个普天同庆的日子。天主教与东正教举行圣诞弥撒，新教举行圣诞礼拜。有些教会的庆祝活动从午夜零点就开始。除崇拜仪式外，还演出圣诞剧，表演耶稣降生的故事。

西方人以红、绿、白三色为圣诞色，圣诞节来临时家家户户都要用圣诞色来装饰。红色的有圣诞花和圣诞蜡烛。绿色的是圣诞树。它是圣诞节的主要装饰品，用砍伐来的杉、柏一类呈塔形的常青树装饰而成。上面悬挂着五颜六色的彩灯、礼物和纸花，还点燃着圣诞蜡烛。

红色与白色相映成趣的是圣诞老人,他是圣诞节活动中最受欢迎的人物。西方儿童在圣诞夜临睡之前,要在壁炉前或枕头旁放上一只袜子,等候圣诞老人在他们入睡后把礼物放在袜子内。在西方,扮演圣诞老人也是一种习俗。

圣诞树 Christmas Tree:

据称,圣诞树最早出现在古罗马12月中旬的农神节,德国传教士尼古斯在公元8世纪用纵树供奉圣婴。随后,德国人把12月24日作为亚当和夏娃的节日,在家放上象征伊甸园的"乐园树",上挂代表圣饼的小甜饼,象征赎罪;还点上蜡烛,象征基督。到16世纪,宗教改革者马丁·路德·为求得一个满天星斗的圣诞之夜,设计出在家中布置一颗装着蜡烛的圣诞树。

圣诞卡 Christmas Card：

世界上第一张圣诞卡是1843年英国人亨利.高乐爵士提议，由约翰.卡尔葛荷斯利设计的。卡片上画的是一个贵族家庭，三代人一齐举杯对一位不在场的亲友表示祝贺。当时他印了1000张，没有用完的印刷厂就以每张1先令的价钱卖出。圣诞卡就这样诞生了。

圣诞老人 Santa Claus：

圣诞老人原指公元4世纪时小亚细亚专区的主教尼古拉，他因和蔼可亲慷慨济贫万里闻名。到了6世纪，东方把他尊称为圣尼古拉。由于民间有关尼古拉的传说中，都联系到少年儿童和礼物，从此，圣诞老人便成为专门在圣诞节向孩子们送礼物的慈祥老人的形象。到了18世纪，通过文学和绘画，圣诞老人逐渐成为身穿红外衣的白胡子、白眉毛老人形象。现在，圣诞老人已经成为圣诞节最受喜爱的象征和传统。他赶着驯鹿，拉着装满玩具和礼物的雪橇挨家挨户给每个孩子送礼物的快乐老精灵的形象已深深地留在人们的记忆中。

圣诞礼物 Christmas Gift：

据《圣经》记载，来自东方的圣人在耶稣降生的时候赠送礼物，这就是圣诞老人为儿童赠送礼品习俗的由来。英国孩子在圣诞前夕把长统袜子放在壁炉旁，相信圣诞老人在夜里会从大烟囱下来，给他们带来满袜子的礼物。法国的孩子把鞋放在门口，让圣婴来时把礼物放在鞋里面。

圣诞大餐 Christmas Dinner：

正像国人过春节吃年夜饭一样，欧美人过圣诞节也很注重全家团聚，围坐在圣诞树下，共进节日美餐。圣诞大餐吃火鸡的习俗始于 1620 年，火鸡烤制工艺复杂，味道鲜美持久，以致麦兜小朋友垂涎三尺。这种风俗盛于美国。英国人的圣诞大餐是烤鹅，而非火鸡。奥大利人爱在平安夜里，全家老小约上亲友成群结队地到餐馆去吃一顿圣诞大餐，其中，火鸡、腊鸡、烧牛仔肉和猪腿必不可少，同时伴以名酒，吃得大家欢天喜地。

Other Celebrations and Observances 其他庆祝活动和惯例仪式

There are many commonly observed celebrations in the United States that are not federal holidays. Some of these observances honor groups of people, such as National African American History Month and Women's History Month, or causes, such as National Oceans Month and National Substance Abuse Prevention Month. Many of these holidays and observances are proclaimed by the President every year.

These are some of the most popular American celebrations and observances that occur every year.

Groundhog Day 土拨鼠日

Groundhog Day is February 2th and has been celebrated since 1887. On Groundhog Day, crowds gather in Punxsutawney, Pennsylvania, to see if groundhog Punxsutawney Phil sees his shadow after emerging from his burrow, thus predicting six more weeks of winter weather. When they first started this tradition, a small number of people would gather to see if Phil would see his shadow. Today, more than 50,000 people gather in a very small town to see if Phil will predict another six weeks of winter or if spring is right around the corner.

Valentine's Day 情人节

Valentine's Day is celebrated on February 14th. The day was named after an early Christian martyr, and on Valentine's Day, Americans give presents like candy or flowers to the ones they love. The first mass-produced valentine cards were sold in the 1840s. This is the official day of love. Children give valentines to each other at school. Whoever has the most valentines at the end of the day can consider him or herself to be the most popular person in the class. Flower shops, candy stores, card shops and restaurants make a lot of money on this one day. This is also the time when young couples become engaged, so the jewelry stores do a lot of business.

Earth Day 世界地球日

Earth Day is observed on April 22th. First celebrated in 1970 in the United States, it inspired national legislation such as the Clean Air and Clean Water Acts. Earth Day is designed to promote ecology, encourage respect for life on earth, and highlight concern over pollution of the soil, air, and water. Earth Day in the US is not overly popular today. Environmental groups try to make it seem important, but only a small amount of clubs will get involved. For most Americans, Earth Day passes by without any notice.

Arbor Day 植树节

National Arbor Day was proclaimed as the last Friday in April by President Richard Nixon in 1970. A number of state Arbor Days are observed at other times of the year to coincide with the best tree planting weather. The observance began in 1872, when Nebraska settlers and homesteaders were urged to plant trees on the largely treeless plains. Arbor Day is a day when various school-sponsored clubs plant trees. On the local level, this day is commemorated by taking a few pictures of people planting trees along a road, in a field, etc.

Mother's Day 母亲节

Mother's Day is the second Sunday of May. President Woodrow Wilson issued a proclamation in 1914 that started the holiday. He asked Americans to give a public expression of reverence to mothers on this day. Carnations have come to represent Mother's Day, following President

William McKinley's habit of always wearing a white carnation, his mother's favorite flower. On Mother's Day family members gather to honor their mother. They might take her out to dinner; buy her some flowers or candy. The importance of Mother's Day is to honor all mothers and express love for them. Restaurants, floral shops and candy companies do a lot of business on this day.

Flag Day 美国国旗纪念日

Flag Day, celebrated on June 14th, has been a presidentially proclaimed observance since 1916. Although Flag Day is not a federal holiday, Americans are encouraged to display the flag outside their homes and businesses on this day to honor the history and heritage the American flag represents. You will see flags everywhere on this day. Some Americans leave their flags up all year long.

Father's Day 父亲节

Father's Day celebrates fathers every third Sunday of June. Father's Day began in 1909 in Spokane, Washington, when a daughter requested a special day to honor her father, a Civil War veteran who raised his children after his wife died. The first presidential proclamation honoring fathers was issued in 1966 by President Lyndon Johnson.

Patriot Day 爱国日

September 11th, 2001, was a defining moment in American history. On that day, terrorists hijacked four commercial airliners to strike targets in the United States. Nearly 3,000 people died as a consequence of the attacks. Patriot Day and National Day of Service and Remembrance are observed on September 11th in honor of the victims of these attacks. You will see and hear many stories about 9/11th and how people are observing it. The media in the US will spend a lot of time reminding people of this day and what happened on it. Usually the President will give a speech on television about the events of this day and that the people who were killed are still on the minds of the American people.

Halloween 万圣节

Halloween is celebrated on October 31th. On Halloween, American children dress up in funny or scary costumes and go 'trick or treat' by knocking on doors in their neighborhood. The neighbors are expected to respond by giving them small gifts of candy or money. On the university campus, parties and events will happen on Halloween. You will be encouraged to put on a costume and have some fun. Lots of dancing, food and music are in store for you. If your university does not allow parties, there will be plenty of parties going on off campus. All the students will know about them. Just listen to what others are saying around you. They will start talking about the parties at least one week in advance. If you want to have a little excitement, visit the local haunted house in the city. It will scare you or make you laugh. Either way, it will be something you will not forget.

Pearl Harbor Day 珍珠港日

Pearl Harbor Remembrance Day is December 7th. In 1994, Congress designated this national observance to honor the more than 2,400 military service personnel who died on this date in 1941, during the surprise attack on Pearl Harbor, Hawaii, by Japanese forces. The attack on Pearl Harbor caused the United States to enter World War II. Military personnel and veterans recall this holiday. Most of the American public seems to let this day pass by.

Ethnic and Religious Holidays 种族和宗教节日

Various ethnic and religious groups in America celebrate days with special meaning to them even though these are not national holidays. For example, Christians celebrate the resurrection of Jesus Christ on Easter, Jews observe their high holy days in September, Muslims celebrate Ramadan, and African Americans celebrate Kwanzaa. There are many other religious and ethnic celebrations in the United States. If you are a religious person, ask others at your school and they can help you with meetings, various churches to attend, etc. If you are not a religious person, don t worry about the holidays. One holiday mentioned in the section is Easter. Easter for university students usually marks the beginning of Spring Break. Spring Break is a 2 week holiday. Students in the north travel to the south or even to other countries to let loose and relax. Some will go as a group to the ski slopes and spend their 2 weeks skiing. Others will go home to relax and have Mom do laundry You will be invited to spend Spring Break somewhere with a friend or group of people. You should go and have a good time.

Spring Break is a big event on the university campus because after January classes begin, there are no major holidays until summer. Everyone takes off and has fun. Give it a try you will be glad you did.

各国传统节日：

1、罗马新年前夕 12 月 31 日

在城市各广场举行传统的岁末庆祝活动，有烟花表演、篝火晚会和摇滚音乐会等。共和国总统将出席在 Piazza del Quirinale 举办的古典音乐会。这天地铁营运到很晚。

2、意大利主显节 1 月 6 日

纪念耶稣显灵的节日，也是意大利的儿童节。传说这天骑着扫帚的巫婆 Befana 从屋顶的烟囱钻进屋里来，把礼物装在靴子里送给小孩。于是，大人们就把给孩子的各种礼物装在长统靴中，放在壁炉上，而淘气的孩子会收到样子象黑炭块的糖。

3、在泰国和缅甸，每年 4 月中旬的泼水节就是他们的新年。

为了欢庆节日，男女老幼都涌上街头，他们有的用银钵、有的用水枪，相互泼水嬉戏，以此传递喜庆吉祥、消灾去病的祝福。讲究的人家还要用银钵盛上浸好玫瑰花瓣的清水，普通人则干脆将整盆整桶的朝路人泼去。不一会儿，大街上人们大都已经浑身湿透了，不过这丝毫没有影响他们的兴致。毕竟，这意味着他们今年又得到了不少的祝福。

4、"开斋节"是穆斯林的重大节日。

尤其是在印尼、巴基斯坦等穆斯林较为集中的国家，开斋节显得尤为隆重。一个月的斋戒之后，人们便可以在开斋节这天随心所欲地品尝各种美味小吃。大人们庆祝节日的同时，小孩子们也不甘寂寞，他们可不肯错过任何可以尽情玩耍的机会。

5、当树叶渐渐变黄，印度北部奈尼达尔每年一度的秋日节也将拉开帷幕。

在秋日节上,印度传统舞蹈"卡塔克舞"当然成了主角。"卡塔克舞"又被称作"铃铛舞",舞者的手腕上和脚踝上系着许多的铃铛。叮叮当当的铃声伴着潇洒的舞步和优美的乐曲,观众们个个心醉神迷,早把秋日落叶引发的伤感情绪远远地抛在了脑后。

6、泰国"鬼节"。

和印度的传统舞蹈相比,泰国这些"妖魔鬼怪"的劲歌热舞似乎更加触目惊心。不用害怕,这是泰国人正在庆祝传统的"鬼节",希望以此祈求风调雨顺、五谷丰登。每年鬼节来临之时,数百名泰国男子就会穿上色彩艳丽的鬼袍、戴上七彩缤纷的鬼面具,伴着鼓声和号角声载歌载舞。在队伍行进过程中,大大小小的妖魔鬼怪们施展浑身解数,不断向围观的人们摆出各种怪异的姿态。置身其中,你很快就会忘记了最初的恐惧感觉,全身心地融入这欢乐的海洋。

7、印度戴维节。

不过,并不是所有的人们都会选用欢乐的方式来庆祝节日。印度传统的戴维节就充斥着一片混乱和打斗的场面。节日当天,数千名印度人分成几个小组,他们手持巨大的盾牌,彼此投掷石头,重演战争场景,模仿英雄皮马河战胜恶魔的壮举。一场战斗下来,不少人都被石头砸得满头大包,满脸流血,只好退下火线,到专门的帐篷医院里坐冷板凳。看看他们的模样真让人于心不忍,但是伤者脸上个个都洋溢着重现英雄壮举的自豪。

8、越南"斗水牛节"

越南每年一度的斗水牛节同样也可以刺激你的视觉神经。在丁丁冬冬的鼓乐声中,已经有1000多年历史的"斗水牛节"又开场了。水牛在场上拼命的同时,水牛的主人们也在心里暗暗地鼓足了劲儿,期待着980美元的优胜者大奖到底会花落谁家。不过,在激烈的比赛中有时也会出现一些意外。有时水牛慌不择路,竟然闯向人群,造成满场一片混乱。

Vocabulary

federal ['fedərəl] adj. 联邦（制）的；美国联邦政府的
approach [ə'prəutʃ] v. 接近；靠近
publication [ˌpʌbli'keiʃən] n. 出版；发表；公布
prosperous ['prɔspərəs] adj. 繁荣的；兴旺的
resolution [rezə'luːʃən] n. 决心
tend [tend] vi. 趋向，倾向
motivated ['motivetid] adj. 有积极性的
clergyman ['klɜːdʒimən] n. 牧师；教士
recognized ['rɛkəg'naizd] adj. 公认的
tireless ['taiəlis] adj. 不知疲倦的；不疲劳的
civil rights 公民权利
nonviolent [ˌnɔn'vaiələnt] adj. 非暴力的
parade [pə'reid] n. 游行；阅兵
convention [kən'venʃən] n. 集会
equality [i'kwɔliti] n. 平等
observed [əb'zɜːvd] v. 纪念，庆祝
legacy ['legəsi] n. 遗赠，遗产
wreath [riːθ] n. 花冠，花环
symbolic [sim'bɔlik] adj. 象征的
grave [greiv] n. 墓穴，坟墓
gravesite [greiv'sait] n. 墓地
departed [di'pɑːtid] v. 离去；去世
adoption [ə'dɑpʃən] n. 采用；接受
picnic ['piknik] n. 野餐
patriotic [ˌpetri'atik] adj. 爱国的

fireworks ['faiəwə:ks] n. 烟花，烟火

display [di'splei] n. 展现；展示；表演

typically ['tipikli] adv. 代表性地；作为特色地

vacation [və'keiʃən] n. 假期

commemorate [kə'meməreit] v. 庆祝，纪念

navigator ['nævigeitə] n. 航海家；领航员

proclaim [prə'kleim] v. 宣告，公布；声明

retailer ['ri:teilə] n. 零售商

promote [prə'məut] vt. 促进；提升；发扬

voyage ['vɔiidʒ] n. 航行；航程

veterans ['vetərənz] n. 老兵；退伍军人

fought [fɔ:t] v. 战斗（fight 的过去分词）

feast [fi:st] n. 筵席，宴会

bountiful ['bauntifʊl] adj. 丰富的；慷慨的

harvest ['hɑ:vist] n. 收获；产量；结果

cranberry ['krænbəri] n. 蔓越莓

inevitably [in'ɛvitəbli] adv. 不可避免地；必然地

invited [in'vaitid] v. 邀请

catching up 赶上，弥补

greeting ['gri:tiŋ] n. 问候；祝贺

commercial [kə'mɜ:ʃəl] adj. 商业的；营利的

exchange [iks'tʃeindʒ] v. 交换

observance [əb'zɜ:vəns] n. 惯例；仪式；庆祝

cause [kɔ:z] n. 原因

groundhog ['graundhɔg] n. 土拨鼠

emerging [i'mɜ:dʒiŋ] v. 显露（emerge 的 ing 形式）

burrow ['bʌrəu] n. （兔、狐等的）洞穴，地道；藏身处

predicting [priˈdiktiŋ] v. 预测（predict 的 ing 形式）；预报；预言

predict [priˈdikt] v. 预报，预言；预知

martyr [ˈmɑːtə] n. 烈士；殉道者

mass-produced [ˌmæsprəˈdjuːst] adj. 大量生产的，大批生产的

whoever [huːˈevə] pron. 无论谁；任何人

engaged [inˈgeidʒd] v. 同…订婚（engage 的过去分词）

jewelry [ˈdʒʊəlri] n. 珠宝；珠宝类

inspired [inˈspaiəd] v. 激发（inspire 的过去分词）；鼓舞

legislation [ledʒisˈleiʃən] n. 立法；法律

ecology [iˈkɔlədʒi] n. 生态学；社会生态学

encourage [inˈkʌridʒ] v. 鼓励；激励；支持

respect [riˈspekt] n. 尊敬，尊重；敬意

highlight [ˈhailait] v. 突出；强调

pollution [pəˈluːʃən] n. 污染

coincide [ˌkəʊinˈsaid] vi. 一致，符合

settler [ˈsetlə] n. 移居者；殖民者

homesteader [ˈhəʊmˌstedə] n. 农场所有人；自耕农

urged [ˈɜːdʒd] vi. 强烈要求

treeless [ˈtrilis] adj. 无树木的

plain [plein] n. 平原

various [ˈveəriəs] adj. 各种各样的；多方面的

school-sponsored 学校发起的，学校赞助的

commemorated [kəˈmeməreitid] v. 庆祝，纪念

proclamation [prɔkləˈmeiʃn] n. 宣告；公布

expression [ikˈspreʃən] n. 表达，表示

reverence [ˈrevərəns] n. 崇敬，尊敬

carnation [kɑːˈneiʃən] n. 康乃馨

importance [im'pɔːtəns] n. 价值；重要性

floral ['flɔrəl] adj. 花的；植物的

presidentially [ˌprezi'denʃəli] adv. 总统（议长，主席）地

flag [flæg] n. 旗子

heritage ['heritidʒ] n. 遗产；传统；继承物

presidential ['prɛzədɛnʃəl] adj. 总统的；首长的

defining [di'fainiŋ] adj. 最典型的；起决定性作用的

terrorist ['tɛrərist] n. 恐怖主义者，恐怖分子

hijacked ['haidʒækt] v. 抢劫，劫机

airliner ['eəlainə] n. 班机；大型客机

strike [straik] v. 打，打击，袭击

target ['tɑːgit] n. 目标；靶子

consequence ['kɔnsikwəns] n. 结果

victim ['viktim] n. 受害人；牺牲者

speech [spiːtʃ] n. 演讲；讲话

scary ['skeəri] adj. 吓人的，可怕的

costume ['kɔstjuːm] n. 服装，装束；戏装，剧装

knocking ['nɔkiŋ] v. 敲（knock 的 ing 形式）

neighborhood ['nebəˌhʊd] n. 附近；街坊

advance [əd'vɑːns] adj. 预先的；先行的

excitement [ik'saitmənt] n. 兴奋；刺激；令人兴奋的事物

haunted ['hɔːntid] adj. 闹鬼的

scare [skeə] v. 惊吓；把…吓跑

attack [ə'tæk] v. 攻击，袭击

ethnic ['eθnik] adj. 种族的；人种的

religious [ri'lidʒəs] adj. 宗教的

resurrection [rezə'rekʃən] n. 复活；恢复；复兴

Ramadan [ˌræməˈdæn] n. 斋月（伊斯兰教历的九月）

Kwanzaa [ˈkwɑːnzə] n. 宽扎节（非裔美国人的节日）

Mentioned [ˈmenʃənd] v. 提到，谈到；提及，论及；说起

loose [luːs] v. 释放，放纵

relax [rɪˈlæks] v. 放松，休息

ski [skiː] v. 滑雪

slope [sləʊp] n. 斜坡

skiing [ˈskiːɪŋ] n. 滑雪运动

laundry [ˈlɔːndri] n. 洗熨

somewhere [ˈsʌmweə] adv. 在某处；到某处

Conversation Questions

1. Will you do anything special during the next holiday?
2. How often do you go home to see your parents?
3. Which holiday is the most special to you?
4. How do you spend Spring Festival?
5. Do you enjoy the fireworks during Spring Festival?
6. What is your favorite memory of a holiday you had in the past?
7. Will you do anything special during the summer vacation time?
8. What kinds of foods do you eat during Spring Festival?
9. Do you help your parents with preparing dinner during the holidays?
10. Are you lazy and relaxed during the holidays?

Discussion Questions

1. Is it more important to spend time with family or friends during the

holiday?

2.What makes a particular holiday so special?

3.Do we need to have so many holidays each year?

4.Why are there more holidays in the fall and winter than in the spring and summer in China?

5.Is there any particular holiday you can do without?

Practice Dialogues

Throughout this book you will have a variety of dialogues that you can use to practice speaking and asking questions. Each section of the book will have 3 dialogues for your use.

Dialogue # 1 – 2 Students

A: So, are you going home during the break?

B: Well, home for me is in China, and a few weeks is not enough time.

A: So what will you do during the 2 weeks off?

B: I will probably stay here and study.

A: Study? Are you crazy?

B: No, I have a lot of research to do for my next paper.

A: Well, that can wait until you get back from your holiday.

B: Like I said, I will probably just stay here and work.

A: No, I think you will go on a nice trip to a small town and have a wonderful time with good friends and good food.

B: Really? How do you figure that will happen?

A: Well, after I invite you all you have to do is say yes.

B: I see. Well, it does sound like a good idea.

A: Nope, I haven't invited you yet.

B: Okay, I will wait until you invite me and then I will say yes.

A: Good. Now, we need to sit down and decide what you need to bring along on the trip.

B: Where are we going?

A: First to my parents home and then on to our cabin by the lake.

B: Oh, that sounds wonderful.

A: It will be a lot of fun. I have invited a few other students to come along too.

B: Are you sure you want me to come?

A: Of course. We all agreed that you should come with us.

B: Great. Let's go plan this trip.

A: All right, that's the spirit!

Dialogue #2 – Student and Professor

S: Excuse me Professor, when do you want us to hand in our research papers?

P: Well, you can hand them in after Spring Break.

S: So, we should be working on our papers throughout Spring Break?

P: No, I think you should relax and enjoy your time out of class.

S: Then what about the paper?

P: I usually give the students 2 weeks after Spring Break to hand in their work.

S: Oh, I see. So there is no rush to get it done before Spring Break or even during Spring Break.

P: Spring Break is a nice time to just relax and enjoy whatever is going on around you. It is a time when students and teachers forget about the classes, the coursework, the exams, and everything connected to school.

S: Okay, I understand. Do you have any special plans for Spring Break?

P: Well, every year I travel to a different place outside the United States.

S: Oh, where will you go this year?

P: I am going to Florence, Italy.

S: Wow! That sounds great.

P: I am visiting some friends who live in Italy, so it will be nice to see them again.

S: Well I hope you have a wonderful time.

P: I hope you enjoy your Spring Break too.

S: I shall. Thanks Professor.

P: You are welcome. See you in a few weeks.

S: Okay.

Dialogue #3- Student and Travel Agent

TA: Guided Tours Travel Agency, how can I help you?

S: I would like to find out how much it would cost to travel this spring to Florida.

TA: Where in Florida do you want to go?

S: Orlando, to Disney World.

TA: And where are you traveling from?

S: New York City.

TA: How would you like to travel? Plane, bus, train?

S: Plane, please.

TA: Okay. When did you plan to leave New York?

S: In about 3 weeks. We have Spring Break coming up.

TA: Yes, that is a very busy time for traveling. Hold on and let me check flights for you.

S: Okay, thank you.

TA: Right, I see a late flight leaving Kennedy Airport at 11pm on Friday the 12th and arriving in Orlando at 3:15am. on Saturday morning. How does that sound?

S: Sounds great. Can you tell me the price?

TA: Certainly. Since it is a late flight, the fare is less. So the price of the ticket is $450.00.

S: What about a return flight?

TA: When do you want to return to New York?

S: Well, I thought I would stay in Orlando for 8 days and then return.

TA: So we are looking at a return flight on the 22nd?

S: No, make it the 23rd.

TA: Okay. Let me check for you.

S: Thanks.

TA: Okay, I have the flight leaving NYC on the 12th at 11pm, arriving in Orlando on the 13th at 3:15am….departing Orlando on the 23rd at 9:00pm and arriving in New York at 12:20am on the 24th. What do you think?

S: Sounds good. What is the total cost for the flight?

TA: Roundtrip ticket this far in advance would be $842.00.

S: Okay, I will take it.

TA: Great. Now let me get your name and number…….

Chapter 6
American Money&Student ID and Passport

美元和学生证/护照问题

Guided Reading

本实训手册最后一部分将对前面章节没有提及到的或需再次强调的内容进行补充说明。内容主要包括美国的钱币、美元和人民币之间的兑换、学生证及护照的重要性和安全问题。

This section of the handbook will look at a few things that you might not know about the US. The topics will vary greatly, so use this section as a reference when you need it.

American Money 美国钱币

美国的钱币和人民币一样，分为硬币和纸币。目前流通的硬币包括:1 美分、5 美分、10 美分、25 美分、50 美分和 1 美元。纸币面额有 1,2, 5,10,20,50 和 100 元。

American money comes in various denominations. Most people in America use the following currency on a daily basis:

Coins 硬币

The coins that are used daily are the penny, nickel, dime and quarter. Other coin currency includes half-dollar, one dollar or silver dollar. Here are some pictures of American currency coins.

Description: The top row is the penny (left 2) and nickel. Second row is the dime (left 2) and quarter. Third row is the one dollar coin. There are two versions of this coin. The back is the same on each, but the front is different. The bottom row is the half dollar.

🎵 Do the Math 算算看？

1 penny is 1/5 of a nickel, 1/10 of a dime, 1/25 of a quarter, 1/50 of a half dollar and 1/100 of a dollar.

100 pennies = 1 dollar

20 nickels = 1 dollar

10 dimes = 1 dollar

4 quarters = 1 dollar

2 half dollars = 1 dollar

Americans use a lot of change throughout the day. It is used to purchase a newspaper, a token for the subway, to buy inexpensive items like candy or junk food or even to ride on the bus. So coins in America are very important and used all the time.

Paper Money 纸币

American currency made of paper is used throughout the world. The currency comes in the following denominations:

One dollar bill, Five dollar bill, Ten Dollar bill, Twenty dollar bill, Fifty dollar bill and One hundred dollar bill

Of course there are higher amounts but those are rarely used by the public. The higher denominations are actually out of circulation and usually owned by collectors. The government stopped printing larger bills in 1969. Below are pictures of the currency used by most Americans today.

One dollar bill with George Washington on the front.

Five dollar bill with Abraham Lincoln on the front.

Ten dollar bill with Thomas Jefferson on the front.

Twenty dollar bill with Andrew Jackson on the front.

Fifty dollar bill with Ulysses S. Grant on the front.

One hundred dollar bill with Benjamin Franklin on the front.

As for the larger currencies that are still circulating, but no longer printed, this is what they look like:

Now that we've completed what American money looks like, where can you get it?

If you are planning to travel to the US, you can exchange Chinese Yuan for US Dollars at the larger Bank of China offices throughout China. There is a fee for exchanging money, but it is minimal. Another place where you can exchange money is at the airport either before you leave China or when you land in the US. In the airports, the exchange rate might be less than the rate offered by the Bank of China. It is your decision to make when you want to exchange money.

Student ID and Passport 学生证及护照的问题

As mentioned earlier in this handbook, once you are registered at the university, you do not need to carry your passport with you. However, you do need to carry your student ID. If you are ill, your student ID will be useful at the local hospital. If you need to do some banking and you are out of town, it is always best to carry your passport with you. Your student ID merely identifies you as a university student. Your passport identifies you as a visitor to the United States. For most travel plans, you need some form of identification with you. To get a bus ticket, you do not. To ride the train, you do not. To book a flight you need your student ID or passport. If you set up travel plans through a travel agency, they will ask for your student ID and passport. One rule for traveling: Never hand over your passport or student ID to anyone. If someone asks for it, allow them to take a photocopy of it. Do not give it to them. You might not get it back.

If you lose your passport while in the US, you need to call the Chinese Embassy to request a new passport. It is quite easy to find the number for the Embassy. All you have to do is look in the local telephone book. All telephone books are set up with different colored pages for easy use. For example, if you need to find a business you look in the yellow pages. If you want to find someone's name, you look in the white pages. If you want to contact a government office, such as the Chinese Embassy, you look in the grey pages. In some cities the grey pages are actually light blue. Knowing what each color represents makes it easier.

Another way to safeguard your passport is to keep a copy of your passport on your computer and a copy of it with your parents. If your computer should crash, you can always have your parents send a copy

to you via the mail service. A suggestion for you is to keep copies of all important papers with your parents for safekeeping. Should any problems arise, you have copies waiting for your use.

One important point to remember as you travel to the United States is that the people in the US are nice and friendly. They will help you if you ask. They will not hurt you. The best thing you can do for your self while in the US is to use common sense. Think before you speak. Lots of times, mistakes that are made come about because the communication was not very clear. This could be the fault of either side. It doesn't matter who is at fault, what does matter is that you should think it out before you speak. In the end common sense will always win.

美元是美国的官方货币,其货币史最早可追溯到1690年。美国在《独立宣言》发表以前,就已经使用纸钞了。作为储备货币,美元在美国以外的国家广泛使用。目前市场上流通的美元纸币是自1929年以来发行的各版钞票,是由美国联邦储备系统控制。从1913年起美国建立联邦储备制度,发行联邦储备券。现行流通的货币中99%以上为联邦储备券。美元的发行主管部门是国会,具体发行业务由联邦储备银行负责办理。美元是外汇交换中的基础货币,也是国际支付和外汇交易中的主要货币,在国际外汇市场中占有非常重要的地位。

美元标志"$"是怎么产生的呢?有许多说法,其中较为普遍的一种说法认为,这个符号是将一个较窄的U放在一个较宽的S上形成的,所以它代表了美国(United States)的美元符号。另一种说法认为,它是PS叠合写法的演变。PS是18至19世纪期间美国的一种圆形硬币比索(Pesos)的缩写,这种硬币在1974年美国正式建立造币厂以前一直在全国通用。后来美国政府认可了$作为新货币的一个单位,即一美元。在书写时,$要摆在数字前面。如1美元应写成$1.100美元写成$100。

美元对人民币汇率走势图

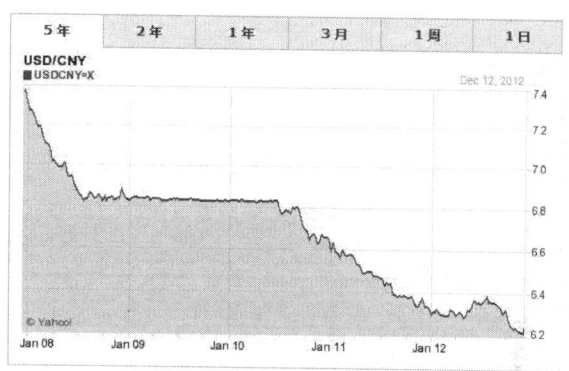

（本图表来自于 http://www.zhijinwang.com/huilv/）

2007年1月1日实施的《中华人民共和国护照法》规定：

第十一条　有下列情形之一的，护照持有人可以按照规定申请换发或者补发护照：

（一）护照有效期即将届满的；

（二）护照签证页即将使用完毕的；

（三）护照损毁不能使用的；

（四）护照遗失或者被盗的；

（五）有正当理由需要换发或者补发护照的其他情形。

护照持有人申请换发或者补发普通护照，在国内，由本人向户籍所在地的县级以上地方人民政府公安机关出入境管理机构提出；在国外，由本人向中华人民共和国驻外使馆、领馆或者外交部委托的其他驻外机构提出。定居国外的中国公民回国后申请换发或者补发普通护照的，由本人向暂住地的县级以上地方人民政府公安机关出入境管理机构提出。

外交护照、公务护照的换发或者补发，按照外交部的有关规定办理。

Vocabulary

denomination[di,namə'neʃən] n. 面额

penny['pɛni] n. 便士；（美国、加拿大的）一分钱

nickel['nikəl] n. [化] 镍；五分镍币

dime [daim] n. （美国、加拿大的）10 分铸币

quarter['kwɔrtɚ] n. （美国或加拿大的）25 分硬币

currency ['kɚrənsi] n. 货币

versions ['vɚʒən, -ʃən] n. 版本

junk [dʒʌŋk] n. 便宜货

circulation [,sɚkjə'leʃən] n. 流通

minimal ['minəməl] adj. <正式> 最小的，极少的

identification [ai,dɛntəfi'keʃən] n. 鉴定，识别；验明

photocopy ['fotə,kɑpi] v. 影印，照相复制；复印

embassy['ɛmbəsi] n. 大使馆

safeguard ['sef,gɑrd] v. 保护，保卫；防护

arise[ə'raiz] v. 产生；出现

Closing Thoughts 总结

I hope this handbook will be of use to you and that it will assist you as you travel to the US. I hope your education in the US is something you will look back on with fond memories. Good luck to you as your journey begins.

Appendix A
Dialogues

生活篇场景对话攻略

场景 1: Student Activities

Dialogue # 1 – 2 Students

A: So, are you going to join any clubs this year?

B: I'm not sure. I've never been in a club before.

A: Really?

B: Yes, at my former school we had no time for clubs.

A: Well, that will change. What interests do you have?

B: Well, I like photography, swimming and reading.

A: Okay. There is a photography club forming on Tuesdays at 6pm in the library. The sign says anyone can join.

B: That sounds good. And it is after my late class on Tuesdays and I would still have time for dinner.

A: Here's one about swimming. They call themselves the Swimeroos. What a silly name!

B: What does it say about swimming?

A: They meet at the gym on Wednesdays at 6:30pm. They participate in local swimming competitions with other colleges and universities. They are part of the Intramural Program. It also says it is co-ed.

B: Hmm. Competitions? I'm not too sure about that one.

A: You don't have to compete to be in the club. The people that go are there to swim and have fun. If some are more competitive than the others, they can do the competition. I think you should give it a try.

B: Well, I do love to swim. And it would be good to meet more people on campus. Okay, you talked me into it.

A: I see a sign for the Literary Guild. They meet every other Thursday at 7pm. in the library. This group discusses the latest works being published today. That sounds interesting. I might even join that group.

B: Great. We can both join then.

Dialogue #2 – Student and Professor

S: I came in to speak to you about the Literary Guild.

P: Yes, what would you like to know?

S: Well, I enjoy reading a great deal, but I also enjoy writing. I have been writing poetry for 4 years now and I want to know if there is a Poetry Club on campus?

P: Well, there is no Poetry Club on campus, but that doesn't mean we can't start one.

S: Well, how would we start a new club?

P: You would need to go to the Student Government Association and get a form for a new club.

S: Okay. Then what do I do? Fill it out?

P: yes, and no. Eventually you will fill out the form, but there are a few others things you need to do as well.

S: Such as?

P: You need to have at least 15 students sign up to begin the club. You need to find a space in which you can hold meetings. You need to elect officers to run the club and you need to get an academic advisor to supervise the club.

S: Gosh, that's a lot of stuff just to open a new club.

P: If you are passionate about your poetry and you want to share it with others, you need to decide if the paperwork and legwork is worth it.

S: I think it is. However, I do not know of an academic advisor who would be willing to supervise the club.

P: Luckily for you, you are speaking to a poet. I would be happy to be the advisor for the club.

S: Really? Wonderful! Well, I will go and get the form and get everything done within this week. Is that okay with you?

P: That would be fine. When you have all the students signed up, bring everything to my office. I will look over everything and then we will start the Poetry Club.

Dialogue #3 – 2 Students

A: I have a full schedule this semester.

B: Really? How many credits are you taking?

A: 18 credits plus 2 labs.

B: Wow! That's 20 credits in total. You must be really organized.

A: Well, I like to stay busy. I don't enjoy having idle time.

B: Most students would be just the opposite….they only want a few classes and more time to sleep or play computer games.

A: I was taught to keep active, so that is what I am doing.

B: What do you do in your spare time?

A: I have a few clubs that I belong to.

B: You have time to be in clubs?

A: Sure. I have a system when it comes to homework, and after it is completed, I have time to go to my clubs.

B: I see. What clubs are you in?

A: I am in the Biology Club, Poetry Club and Swimming Club.

B: I am amazed. I am taking 15 credits this semester and I barely have time to finish my studies and have dinner. How do you do it?

A: It all depends on how organized you are and how disciplined you are.

B: Meaning?

A: For me, club activities do not happen if I have a research paper or big exam to study for. Class work always comes first. I use the clubs as a bonus for finishing my tasks.

B: Oh, sort of like a reward for good behavior or for making good grades.

A: Yes, exactly.

B: So, can you help me get myself organized?

A: Of course. It is not difficult to do, but you must be willing to make some compromises as you go along.

B: Okay. I can compromise on anything as long as I have better grades.

A: Great. Let's get started.

B: Okay.

场景 2：Getting Around the City or Town

Dialogue # 1 – 2 Students

A: Would you like to go downtown with me this afternoon?

B: Sure, what time do you want to go?

A: Well, I was thinking of going after my English class, around 2 o'clock.

B: That's sounds good. I have a math class that finishes at 1:45.

A: Great. Let's meet back at the dorm and then go from there.

B: Okay. I will be ready when you get back from class.

A: Oh, make sure you wear sports shoes.

B: Why?

A: Because we will be doing a lot of walking.

B: Good. I enjoy walking.

A: And I will show you some of the city. I will be your guide.

B: That sounds like fun. Can I bring my camera along?

A: Sure. I can take you to some very famous sites and you can have your picture taken there.

B: I would like that. I want to send some home to my parents and friends.

A: No problem. So, I will see you here at 2pm.

B: Sounds great. See you then.

A: Bye

B: Bye, have fun in English.

Dialogue #2 – Same 2 Students

A: See that building? I was built 3oo years ago. It is one of the oldest buildings in America.

B: Hmm. 300 years is not really that old.

A: Well, if you think about it, America is not an old country, so 300 years in a young country seems old.

B: I guess you are right. In China, we see old buildings all the time. We have a history that goes back over 5,000 years.

A: Wow! Did you have to study the history of China when you were growing up?

B: Not really, but we did have some classes in it.

A: That's a lot of information to study. I'm glad I never had to do that.

B: The history of China is so long, that most schools only look at the dynasties and the history of their region. China is too large for anyone to remember all the historical things that happened around the country.

A: That makes sense. In America we are required to study our state history, and students who major in history take classes that cover all of American history.

B: What is that over there?

A: That is one of our most famous sites. Let's get off the bus and go see it.

B: Okay, you go first, I will follow you.

A: This is the Metropolitan Museum of Modern Art. Inside are famous pieces of art, sculpture and even manuscripts from famous artists around the world.

B: Oh I love art. Can we go in?

A: Sure. Are you ready?

B: Yes.

A: Oh, before we go in, there are some areas inside where you can't take a picture. The flash of the camera might damage the paintings. There are signs posted. You'll see.

B: Thanks for telling me beforehand.

A: Let's go.

B: Okay.

A: We are in luck. They have the Mona Lisa on display this month. It was brought over from France.

B: The REAL Mona Lisa?

A: Yep. This museum is one of the best in the world. It ranks at the top with the Louvre in Paris.

B: Wow!

A: Shall we go see her?

B: Yes, please. I want to say that I actually looked at Mona Lisa.

A: This way.

Dialogue #3 – Student and RA

RA: I heard you went to the museum today. Did you like it?

S: Oh yes, it was really exciting.

RA: What part did you like the most?

S: I would have to say that looking at the Mona Lisa was the best part.

RA: Really? When I saw it I was disappointed.

S: Why? It is such a masterpiece.

RA: Yes, but I had to wait in line for such a long time and when I finally got up to see it, it was locked behind a wall and I had to look in that little hole of glass to see it.

S: Now that you mention it, I did stand a while to see it. I was a little disappointed because it wasn't just there hanging on the wall. But thinking back on the day, it was the highlight.

RA: Did you get any pictures?

S: Oh yes, I have a ton of pictures to download and send back home.

RA: Good. Make sure you take lots of pictures when you are in the city.

S: Why is that?

RA: Well, you never know who you might meet. It could be a movie start or some important politician.

S: Have you ever met a movie star?

RA: Not personally, but I've seen a few having dinner or walking on the street.

S: That must have been exciting for you.

RA: Yes, it was, but I did not have my camera with me, so I couldn't take a picture. Besides, they have their pictures taken all the time.

S: Well they are starts, so they should be used to that.

RA: Sure, but I think they also like to have privacy.

S: That makes sense; being in front of a camera, making a movie for others to enjoy. I guess they would like some private time without pictures being taken.

RA: Well, just make sure you always have your camera with you so you can get some good pictures for your parents and friends to see in China.

S: I will.

RA: Time for me to do some studying. Have a good evening.

S: Thanks, time for me to study also. Good night.

RA: Good night.

场景 3: Dining Out

Dialogue # 1 – Student and the RA

S: Hi. Can I ask you a few questions?

RA: Sure. What do you want to know?

S: Well, a few of us are going out to eat next week because it is my birthday.

RA: Well, happy birthday.

S: Thanks so much. I have not been to a restaurant off campus and I want to know about a few that might be near the school.

RA: Well, there are many restaurants near the campus. What kind of food do you want to try?

S: I'm not sure. There are 2 of us from China and 1 from Sweden. The others are from America. About 6 people will go to dinner and they all have different tastes for food.

RA: Let me see. Come to my office, I have some things that might make it easier for you.

S: Okay.

RA: Here are the menus for some places near the campus. You can actually walk to any of them with no problems. It would take you about 10 minutes to get there.

S: Great. Can I share these with the other students?

RA: Sure. But when you are finished, make sure you bring them back to me. I use them to plan a party at the end of the semester before summer starts.

S: Oh that sounds like fun.

RA: It is a lot of fun, but a lot of work too. I think you will enjoy it when it comes around.

S: Me? Oh I am sure I will enjoy it. Thanks for the menus. I will bring them back soon.

RA: Okay. If your birthday party is next week, you might think about calling and making a reservation. The restaurants near the campus are always busy. It would be much easier for your group if you have a reservation set up.

S: Thanks for the suggestion. I will call once we decide where we are going.

RA: Okay. See you later then.

S: Right and thanks again for your help.

RA: No problem.

Dialogue #2 – Student /Restaurant Phone Call

R: Michael's Restaurant, can I help you?

S: Yes, I would like to make a reservation, please?

R: Okay, let me get some information from you.

S: Okay.

R: Now the, what is your last name?

S: My last name is _____.

R: Okay. And how many people are in your party?

S: 6 people.

R: Good. Now what day would you like to make the reservation for?

S: I would like it for a week from this coming Friday.

R: So, next week on Friday?

S: Yes.

R: And what time would you like to come to the restaurant?

S: We would like to set the reservation for 7pm.

R: Okay. Do you want to sit inside or outside?

S: Gee, I didn't know you had seating outside. Let me think for a second.

R: Take your time, no rush.

S: Thank you. Hmmm, I think we will sit inside.

R: Very good. So let me read back your reservation to you.

S: Okay.

R: That is a reservation for _____, a party of 6 for next Friday at 7pm inside the restaurant. Correct?

S: Yes, that's right.

R: Great. Is there anything else I can help you with?

S: I'm not sure. I am planning the party because it is my birthday and I want it to be special since this is my first time in America.

R: Oh well, everything will be taken care of next Friday. Do not worry, it's your birthday and it should be a special occasion.

S: Thank you for your help. We will see you next week.

R: Okay. Have a good weekend, see you next week.

Dialogue #3 – At the Restaurant

Hostess (H): Good evening and welcome to Michael's. Do you have a reservation?

S: Yes, the reservation is under the name _____.

H: Oh yes, a party of 6?

S: Yes, that's right.

H: Follow me please.

S: Thank you.

H: Here's your table. Please have a seat. Your waiter will be over soon.

S: Thank you.

W: Hello, my name is David. I will be your waiter this evening.

S: Hi David.

W: Would you like any drinks from the bar?

S: Yes, we would like a large pitcher of beer, please.

W: Very good. While I am getting your drinks, please look through the menu. If you look over there on the wall you can see the specials we have for this evening. I will answer any questions you have when I return with your drinks.

S: Okay, thanks.

W: Now, what would you like to order?

S: I think we want to order 3 of your specials: the extra large pizza, the cheese bread and the pasta salad.

W: Sounds good. Is there anything else you want to order?

S: No, not right now.

W: Very well, I will put your order in.

S: Thank you David.

W: My pleasure.

W: Here is your extra large pizza, bread and pasta salad. Enjoy your meal.

S: Thanks.

W: Would anyone care for dessert or coffee?

S: I'm not sure. Give us a moment to talk about it.

W: No problem. Just wave and I will come to you.

S: David we would like some tea please.

W: Green tea? Red tea? Black tea?

S: Green tea would be nice.

W: I will bring 2 pots of tea for the table.

S: Great. Thank you.

W: According to the hostess and manager, it is your birthday today. So the staff would like to give you this birthday cake and we all wish you a very

happy birthday.

S: Wow! Thank you so much. It looks so good. Can I give you a piece of the cake David?

W: Sure, if you wish. I can eat it later when I am on break.

S: Well here. Take this piece and enjoy it.

W: Thank you very much.

S: Thank you David. This has turned out to be a wonderful birthday.

场景 4: Contacts and facing problems/solving problems

Dialogue # 1 – Student and the RA

S: Hi, can I talk to you for a minute?

RA: Sure, come on in.

S: Thanks. I need to change a class but I don't know how. Can you help me?

RA: No problem. What class are you changing?

S: I need to change my English class from 8am to the 10am class.

RA: Is there a reason why you want to change classes?

S: Not really, except all my classes begin at 10am except the English one.

RA: Oh, so you want to sleep in on that day instead of having to get up early for the class?

S: I guess so.

RA: Have 2 weeks passed since classes began?

S: No, we have a few more days left in this week. Why?

RA: The policy for changing classes is that you can do so within the first 2 weeks of classes. You don't have to give a reason for the change, you simply have to fill out the add/drop form in the registrar's office.

S: Oh, so I have to go to the Registrar's Office, fill out the add/drop form and hand it in?

RA: Yep. Make sure you take along your student ID so they can change it quickly for you.

S: Great! Thanks for your help.

RA: Oh, one other thing. When you change classes, make sure who the new teacher is. He/she might have a different book for you to use. That would mean a trip over to the bookstore to buy another book.

S: Oh, not a problem. It's the same teacher. She said it would be no problem for me to change.

RA: well then, you are all set to go.

S: thanks again for your help. I appreciate it.

RA: Any time. See you later.

S: Bye.

Dialogue #2 – Student at Registrar's Office

Clerk: Next?

S: Hi. I want to change classes.

Clerk: Have you filled out the add/drop slip?

S: Yes, I have.

Clerk: Okay, everything looks good. Can I see your ID card?

S: Sure, here you go.

Clerk: Okay, let me check everything in the computer. Alright, you have

been changed to the 10am English class. Same teacher, same classroom.

S: Thank you.

Clerk: No problem. Just remember, if you want to change classes do it before the 2 week deadline.

S: What happens if I wait until after the 2 weeks is up?

Clerk: Well, there is a lot of paperwork involved. You have to speak to the professors and get permission from them. We have to call them and verify everything. It takes a while to process everything. The worst part is that the professors don't have to let you in their class. They begin classes and cover all the rules in the first few days. Then they hand out assignments. For a student to come in to the class later than 2 weeks means that student is behind at the start. So professors have to make the decision to let a student in or not.

S: I understand.

Clerk: If you want to change classes, make sure you are doing it for the right reasons.

S: Got it. Thanks for the help and the advice.

Clerk: Not at all. Have a great semester.

Dialogue #3 – Student and Professor

P: So, I understand you wish to drop my morning class and move to my 10am class?

S: Yes, ma'am.

P: Why do you want to change classes?

S: Well, your class is the only one on my schedule for 8am.

P: Oh, so you want to sleep in instead of getting up and coming to my class?

S: Yes and no.

P: What do you mean, yes and no?

S: Yes, I want to get more sleep, but I prefer to be more organized. My schedule is all set up with 10am classes except yours. I think it would be better if I had all 10am classes.

P: or 8am classes.

S: Well, yes.

P: So, are you always like this? This predictable? This calculated?

S: I guess I am. Why?

P: You are coming from another country to the US. You are also in a university and things are not always predictable or calculated here. Want some advice?

S: Yes, please.

P: Try to be less organized, especially when it comes to your schedule.

S: So you are saying I should be more flexible?

P: Right. When you study for your classes, you can be as organized as you wish. But setting up a schedule should not be rigid or set in stone. University life is not like school back in your country. We do not require students to be up at a certain hour or in bed at a certain hour. We put that responsibility on you. So keep your schedule loose. Allow things to happen during the day and eventually you will find that your days are filled with different happenings.

S: I see what you mean. However, I do have one question for you.

P: Okay, what is your question?

S: Can I loosen up my schedule next semester and just move from your 8am class to your 10am class for now?

P: Of course. Only if you promise to change your schedule up next semester.

S: I promise.

P: Okay, now you need to head to the Registrar's Office to fill out the add/drop form for class changes.

S: Thank you for your time.

P: Not at all. My office hours are set for a reason.

S: Good bye. See you in class tomorrow.

P: I certainly hope so.

场景 5: American Holidays

Dialogue # 1 – 2 Students

A: So, are you going home during the break?

B: Well, home for me is in China, and a few weeks is not enough time.

A: So what will you do during the 2 weeks off?

B: I will probably stay here and study.

A: Study? Are you crazy?

B: No, I have a lot of research to do for my next paper.

A: Well, that can wait until you get back from your holiday.

B: Like I said, I will probably just stay here and work.

A: No, I think you will go on a nice trip to a small town and have a wonderful time with good friends and good food.

B: Really? How do you figure that will happen?

A: Well, after I invite you all you have to do is say yes.

B: I see. Well, it does sound like a good idea.

A: Nope, I haven't invited you yet.

B: Okay, I will wait until you invite me and then I will say yes.

A: Good. Now, we need to sit down and decide what you need to bring along on the trip.

B: Where are we going?

A: First to my parents home and then on to our cabin by the lake.

B: Oh, that sounds wonderful.

A: It will be a lot of fun. I have invited a few other students to come along too.

B: Are you sure you want me to come?

A: Of course. We all agreed that you should come with us.

B: Great. Let's go plan this trip.

A: All right, that's the spirit!

Dialogue #2 – Student and Professor

S: Excuse me Professor, when do you want us to hand in our research papers?

P: Well, you can hand them in after Spring Break.

S: So, we should be working on our papers throughout Spring Break?

P: No, I think you should relax and enjoy your time out of class.

S: Then what about the paper?

P: I usually give the students 2 weeks after Spring Break to hand in their work.

S: Oh, I see. So there is no rush to get it done before Spring Break or even during Spring Break.

P: Spring Break is a nice time to just relax and enjoy whatever is going

on around you. It is a time when students and teachers forget about the classes, the coursework, the exams, and everything connected to school.

S: Okay, I understand. Do you have any special plans for Spring Break?

P: Well, every year I travel to a different place outside the United States.

S: Oh, where will you go this year?

P: I am going to Florence, Italy.

S: Wow! That sounds great.

P: I am visiting some friends who live in Italy, so it will be nice to see them again.

S: Well I hope you have a wonderful time.

P: I hope you enjoy your Spring Break too.

S: I shall. Thanks Professor.

P: You are welcome. See you in a few weeks.

S: Okay.

Dialogue #3- Student and Travel Agent

TA: Guided Tours Travel Agency, how can I help you?

S: I would like to find out how much it would cost to travel this spring to Florida.

TA: Where in Florida do you want to go?

S: Orlando, to Disney World.

TA: And where are you traveling from?

S: New York City.

TA: How would you like to travel? Plane, bus, train?

S: Plane, please.

TA: Okay. When did you plan to leave New York?

S: In about 3 weeks. We have Spring Break coming up.

TA: Yes, that is a very busy time for traveling. Hold on and let me check flights for you.

S: Okay, thank you.

TA: Right, I see a late flight leaving Kennedy Airport at 11pm on Friday the 12th and arriving in Orlando at 3:15am. on Saturday morning. How does that sound?

S: Sounds great. Can you tell me the price?

TA: Certainly. Since it is a late flight, the fare is less. So the price of the ticket is $450.00.

S: What about a return flight?

TA: When do you want to return to New York?

S: Well, I thought I would stay in Orlando for 8 days and then return.

TA: So we are looking at a return flight on the 22nd?

S: No, make it the 23rd.

TA: Okay. Let me check for you.

S: Thanks.

TA: Okay, I have the flight leaving NYC on the 12th at 11pm, arriving in Orlando on the 13th at 3:15am....departing Orlando on the 23rd at 9:00pm and arriving in New York at 12:20am on the 24th. What do you think?

S: Sounds good. What is the total cost for the flight?

TA: Roundtrip ticket this far in advance would be $842.00.

S: Okay, I will take it.

TA: Great. Now let me get your name and number…….

Appendix B
Word Bank

词汇表

accepted	assume	cashier
accomplishing	atmosphere	casual
accountable	atmosphere	catching up
accustomed	attack	causes
adjustment	authentic	cautious
adoption	await	character
advance	awareness	charity
advantage	bargains	check
advertise	bearings	cheer
advocate	beforehand	cheering
affect	behalf	cheerleading
afraid	behave	chess
airliner	behavior	choreography
alcohol	bill	circulation
alcoholic	Biology	citizens
alerting	boisterous	civil
allergy	bond	civil rights
Anthropology	bountiful	clarification
anticipate	branch out	clergyman
apologize	bread	clinic
appetite	briefcase	clothes
appetizer	buddy	cognizant
appointment	budget	coincide
approach	burrow	collaboration
arise	cafeterias	collaboratively
arrival	canoeing	colleague
aspects	carnation	collegiate

commemorated	credit card	doubt
commemorate	critical	duty
commercial	cultural	Ecology
common sense	curb	ecology
companion	currency	economics
complain	curricular	effectiveness
complete	customary	embassy
complex	daunting	emerging
component	dedicate	encounter
compromise	defining	encourage
concept	delegate	endeavor
confine	delegation	engaged
conflict	delicacy	enhance
consequence	demonstrate	enthusiastic
conservative	denomination	entity
consider	departed	environment
constituency	descent	environment
consumption	dessert	equality
contract	destination	especially
contribute	dictate	especially
convention	dime	essential
convey	diplomacy	establishment
convince	discarded	ethical
correspondence	discipline	ethnic
costume	display	evaluation
cranberry	diverse	eventually
creature	dose	eventually

exchange	fundraiser	inform
excitement	generate	informal
excursion	Geography	inspired
execution	graves	institutional
exhibit	gravesite	intellectual
expectation	greeting	Intention
express	groundhog	interpersonal
expression	guidelines	intramural
facilitate	habit	invited
factor	Happy Hour	jewelry
feast	harvest	joint
federal	haunted	judge
fellowship	heritage	judgment
fertile	highlight	junk
finger food	hijacked	kayaking
firework	homesick	keenly
flag	homesteaders	kitchen
floral	honed	knocking
focal	hospitable	Kwanzaa
focus	identification	laundry
folder	imagine	leadership
forgotten	immigrants	legacy
formal	implementation	legislation
forum	importance	let loose
fought	inevitably	liking
frugal	inevitably	limited funds
functions	inexpensive	located

loose	navigator	personally
loud	negotiation	perspective
mainland	neighborhood	photocopy
maintain	nervous	Physics
manners	newness	pick-pocket
marketing	nickel	picnics
martyr	noise	plains
mass-produced	non-verbal	pleasant
means	nonviolent	pocket
memorable	northern	polite
memories	observances	pollution
mention	observed	predict
mentioned	obtained	predicting
menu	obviously	prepared
merely	obviously	presidential
metropolitan	options	presidentially
minimal	outgoing	pressuring
mission	overall	preventable
mode	overcome	primarily
moment	overly	privately
motivated	overnight	process
motivation	pants	process
multicultural	parades	proclaimed
multiply	passion	proclamation
mutually	pasta	professionalism
natural	patriotic	proficiency
navigate	penny	programmers

project
promote
prosperous
public transportation
publication
pull
purse
pursuing
quarter
quickly fade
quiet
rafting
Ramadan
reaction
reality
reasoned with
recognized
recruitment
regardless
reinvent
relax
relay
relevant
religious
relocate
relying
reservations

reserved
resolution
respect
resurrection
retailers
retention
reverence
risk management
rucksack
safeguard
sales tax
salty
scare
scary
school-sponsored
seeking
seldom
separate
seriously
settlers
situation
situational
ski
skiing
skill set
slopes
smoother

Sociology
solutions
somewhere
southern
special
spectrum
speech
spirit
spoons
spread
stand out
stereotypes
stolen
stolen
stranger
strike
stuck
subsection
suitable
surroundings
symbolic
talkative
targets
taste
tax
tenant
tend

tendency
terrorist
thrifty
tight-knit
tip
tipping
tireless
tolerate
touching
transaction
transferable
treat
treeless
trustworthy
turn down the volume
typically
understandable
unfriendly
unified
unique
unique
unnoticed
urged
utilize
vacation
Valentines Day

valid
valuable
various
vary
vegans
vegetarian
venture
version
veteran
victim
volunteer
voyage
waiter
waiter
waitress
waitress
wallet
watchful
whoever
within
wreath
young